Wired Jewelry

Knitting, crocheting, and twisting in wire

Wired Jewelry

Knitting, crocheting, and twisting in wire

KATH ORSMAN

THE GUILD OF MASTER CRAFTSMAN PUBLICATIONS

To Mum—for a lifetime
of love, support, and
encouragement

First published 2010 by
Guild of Master Craftsman
Publications Ltd
Castle Place,
166 High Street, Lewes,
East Sussex BN7 1XU

Reprinted 2011

ISBN 978-1-86108-699-0

A catalog record for this book
is available from the British Library.

Publisher Jonathan Bailey
Production Manager Jim Bulley
Managing Editor Gerrie Purcell
Senior Project Editor Virginia Brehaut
Copy Editor Kim Davies
Managing Art Editor Gilda Pacitti
Design JC Lanaway
Photography styled photography
by Rebecca Mothersole, step-by-step
pictures by Kath Orsman, and cut-out
photography by Anthony Bailey

Set in Avant Garde and Didot
Color origination by GMC
Reprographics
Printed and bound in China by
Voion Printing Company

Contents

Introduction

The idea of knitting or crocheting using wire may surprise you, but with the minimum of basic skills and some inexpensive materials you can easily produce stunning and unique jewelry.

Knitting and crochet have always been favorite hobbies of mine. Having knitted my way through hundreds of patterns and with the family pleading for no more, I began to experiment with other materials.

Wire was an interesting choice and I plodded through a bracelet project in thick wire—a painful first experience. Undaunted, I experimented and then developed my own designs. I went on to sell my pieces at craft fairs, where they were well received. Eventually, I decided to record my ideas and take on the new challenge of writing a book. I hope you enjoy these projects, and that you are pleased with the results.

From inexpensive materials, you can create beautiful and unique jewelry to be worn with pride. The projects are easy to follow and require only basic knitting and crochet skills. They allow you to make necklaces that will perfectly match your outfit and are unique—when you make your own jewelry, you know that no-one

else will be wearing anything quite like you. Using a minimum of equipment and readily available materials, you can make any of these projects in an evening. The instructions are simple, and step-by-step photographs clearly show how the work will progress to the finished article. Each project includes technical tips to enable you to get a professional finish. The choice of beads and wire color will be very much your own—and I encourage you to be as adventurous as you like.

All of the projects can be added to and adapted. There is a variations section with every project, which provides ideas on how to add your own creative or experimental touches. Bracelets, earrings, chokers, and other items are all possible with slight adaptations to the initial project. Experiment and have fun!

Kath

9

CONFETTI
page 54
Basic beaded knitting

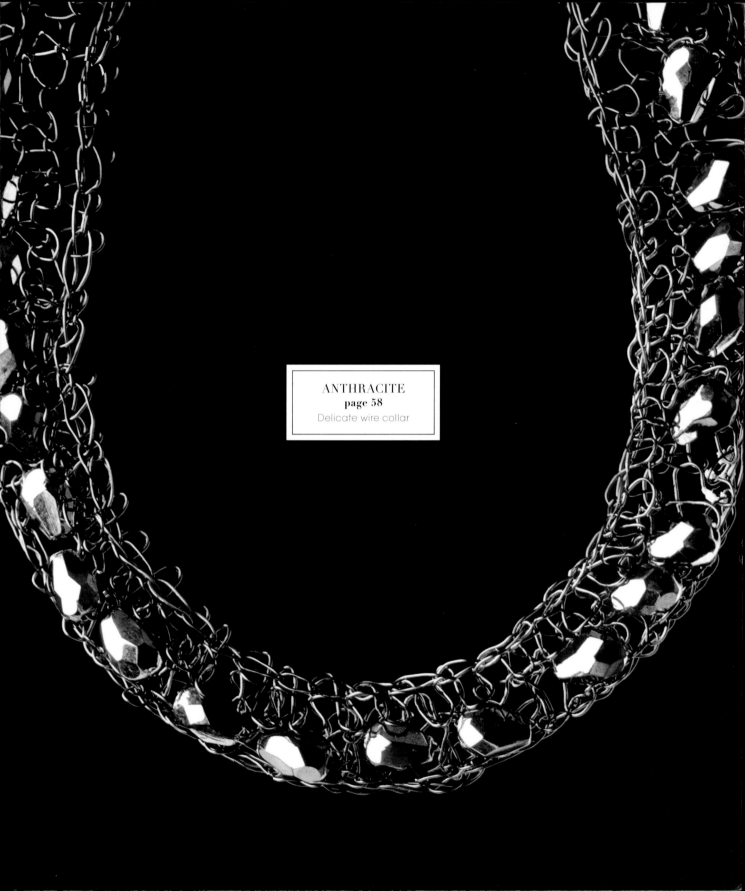

ANTHRACITE
page 58
Delicate wire collar

BAUBLE
page 62
Loop-effect wirework

SPIRAL
page 66
Stylish coiled tube

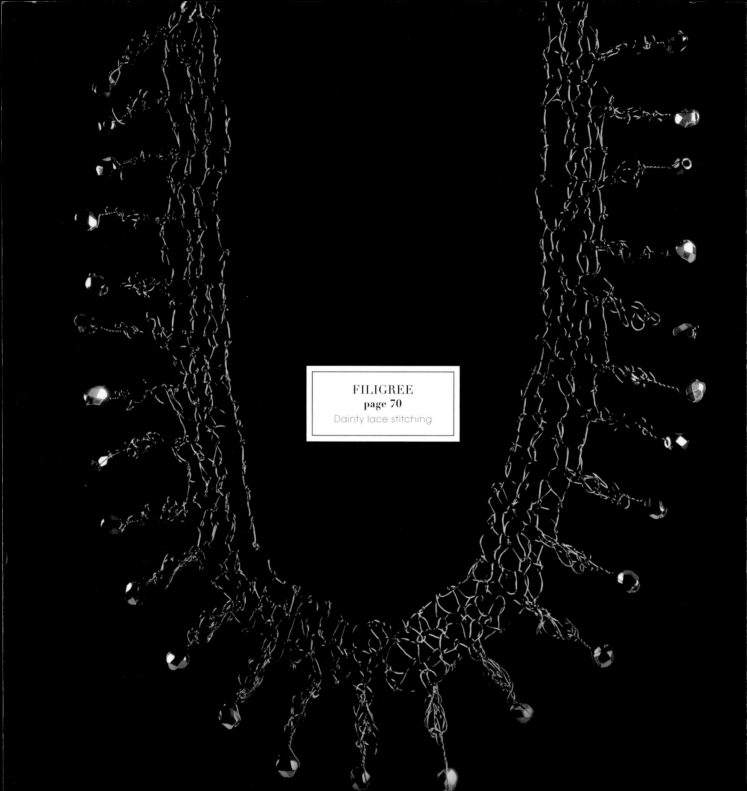

FILIGREE
page 70
Dainty lace stitching

CARBON
page 76
Basic beaded French knitting

GOSSAMER
page 80
Plain plaited chain

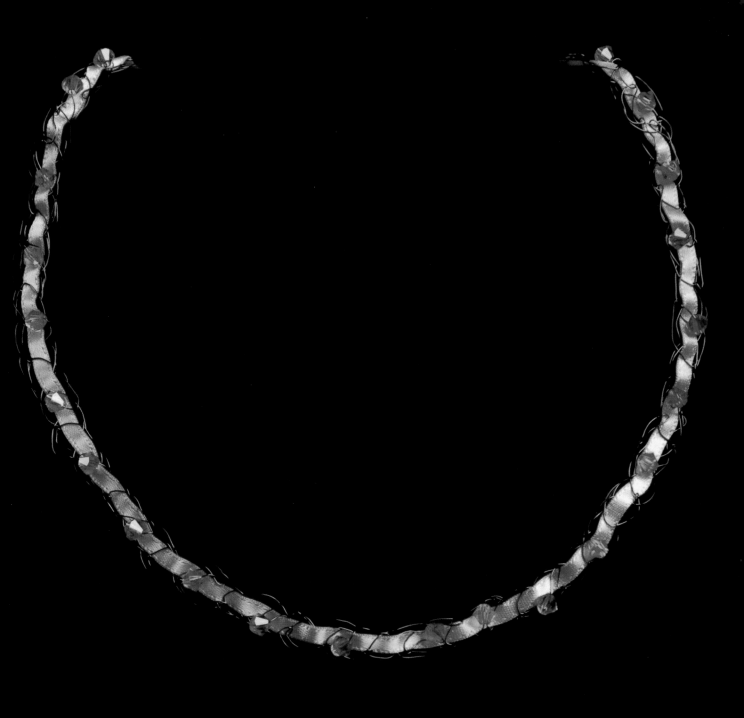

CLEMENTINE
page 84
Pretty ribbon-weave

ELECTRIC
page 88
Two-stranded twisting

COBALT
page 94
Basic beaded crochet

ZEST
page 98
Pretty chain-stitch collar

CLUSTER
page 102
Chunky crochet plait

AZURE
page 106
Dramatic center drop

AQUA
page 110
Crochet-covered beads

LEAF
page 114
Delicate shaped chain

TREE
page 124
Branched-effect twisting

COPPER
page 128
Combined knot and twist

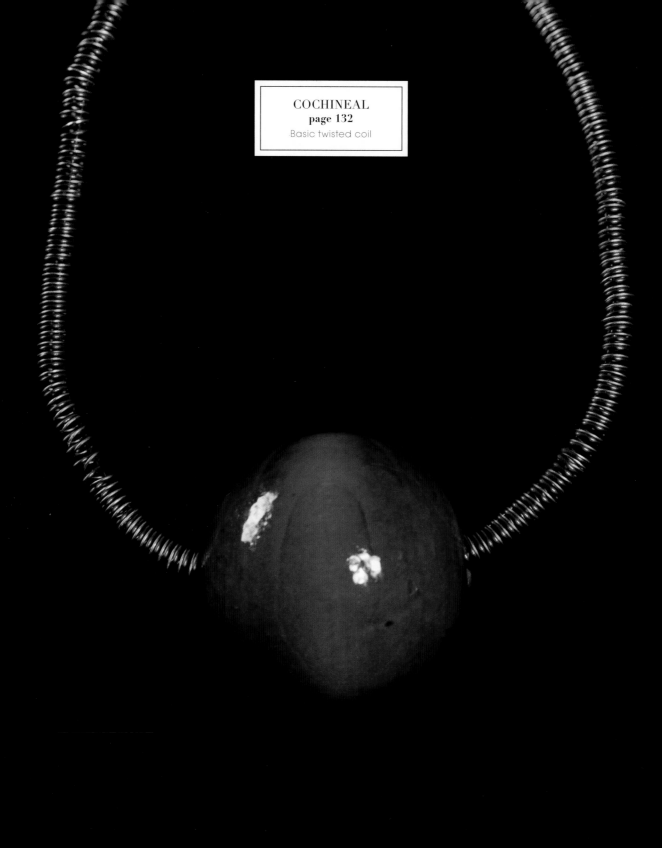

COCHINEAL
page 132
Basic twisted coil

BLOSSOM
page 136
Spiral-effect coil

getting
started

Essential materials

Wire

The wire that you choose needs to be soft enough to bend sufficiently yet strong enough to support the weight of beads that you use.

The projects in this book have all been done in craft wire, which is copper wire with a colored coating. It comes in a beautiful range of colors, and is readily available and inexpensive. The wire also comes in a variety of gauges. For the projects in this book

I have used fine 0.2mm (AWG 32, SWG 36) wire, a slightly heavier 0.25mm (AWG 30, SWG 33) wire, or a medium wire that is 0.315mm (AWG 28, SWG30). Anything much heavier than the medium wire becomes difficult to work with and too hard on the fingers.

Wire can be purchased in hanks or on a reel. Hanks need to be rewound carefully on to a spare cotton reel. Secure with an elastic band.

Beads

There is a huge choice of beads available. Glass beads work well because they have a natural "weight," which means they will sit well on the neck. It is best to avoid foiled beads since they can be rubbed by the wire and lose their shine.

Gemstones have a lovely random nature and work very well in some of the projects in this book. They can be more expensive than glass beads but are often worth the price.

Wooden beads are a good choice, particularly big chunky ones. Again the natural colors are very attractive.

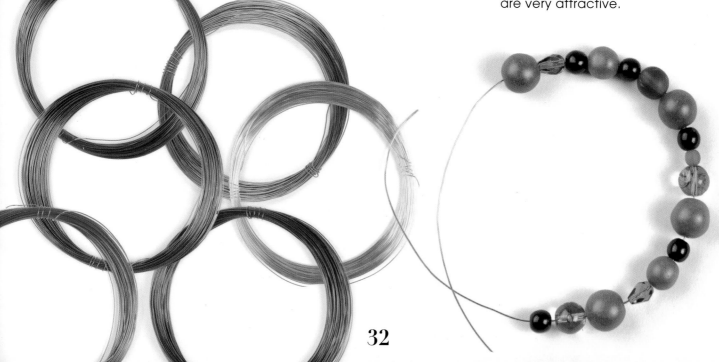

Pearl-effect beads

Gemstone beads

Small glass beads

Some of the projects call for small beads. Seed beads can be useful here, as can long, thin glass beads. Swarovski beads add a lovely sparkle to your work. Look for the ones with AB in the description as these ones have a beautiful iridescent luster.

Metal, ceramic, sequins, gemstone, plastic, pearls and Pandora beads can all be used in wire jewelry. Remember that the beads you use must match the weight of the wire.

Some suppliers offer larger bags of beads (35oz or 1kg), containing a random mixture. These bags are often great value, and offer a good mix of beads to get you started.

Findings

Findings is the name given to all the fastenings and fittings used in jewelry making. The projects in this book call for only a few findings; these are readily available, often from bead suppliers.

Clasps Lobster clasps, round clasps, and magnetic or screw fasteners can all be used. A split ring (which looks like a double ring of wire, or a key ring) or a special clasp is used with lobster and round clasps. The screw and magnetic clasps are best used only with lighter-weight pieces; they are not strong enough for heavy beaded necklaces. Avoid jump rings since the wire can escape through the gap if it is not securely fitted.

These fastenings are all available in both gold and silver colors, and it is useful to have both of these. Check the measurements, and then match the weight of the necklace to the size of clasp.

Crimp beads These are used to secure the wire when you are attaching fastenings. Usually available in gold, silver, and bronze, they come in different sizes. You are likely to use the smaller sizes more often. They take four strands of wire, while the larger ones can be used with ribbon, too.

Glass beads

Ring-and-bar clasps

Screw fastenings

Round clasp

Magnetic fastening

Lobster clasps

Essential materials

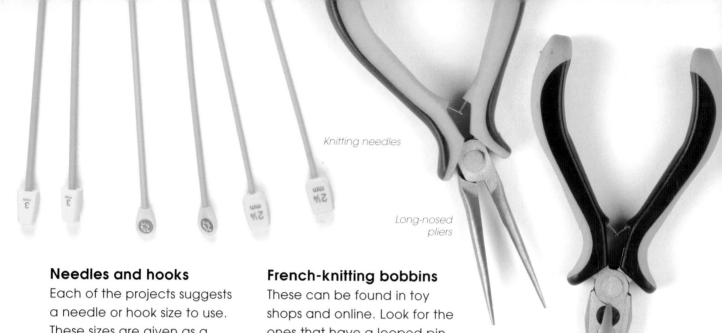

Knitting needles

Long-nosed pliers

Combination pliers

Needles and hooks

Each of the projects suggests a needle or hook size to use. These sizes are given as a guide only; by experimenting with different needle or hook sizes, you can produce quite different finished results.

Wire can be hard on fine knitting needles and they tend to bend in use. Most of the knitted projects work best with short needles that range in size from 2.25mm (USB-1:UK13) to 3.25mm (USB-3:UK10)—any larger and the work becomes more open and flexible. It is best if you can reserve specific needles and hooks for your jewelry making.

French-knitting bobbins

These can be found in toy shops and online. Look for the ones that have a looped pin at the top rather than the nail type. Clear plastic bobbins are best since they enable you to see your work as it progresses. French-knitting bobbins usually come with four pins but three-, six-, and eight-pin ones are also available. Some come with a changeable head, giving you more flexibility. You will need a pointed metal tool to lift the wire over the pins. If the bobbin doesn't come with one, then a cable needle (a short, double-pointed needle) will do the job.

Other tools

You will need pliers; these should be small so you can be accurate in use. Pointed ones are the most useful, and lightweight ones are more comfortable to hold. You do not need wire-cutters—you can use an old pair of scissors to cut the wire. Reserve a pair specially for jewelry making since they will be spoilt for paper cutting.

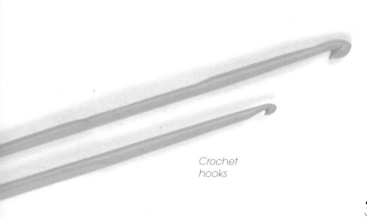

Crochet hooks

French-knitting bobbins

34

Storage and other equipment

Zipped plastic bags

Storage crate

A large, lidded storage crate is very useful for putting all your bits and pieces away neatly and making your projects much more portable.

Plastic tubs

Translucent food containers are excellent for storing your beads. Avoid compartment boxes—they are too small. Square boxes are best since these pack away neatly in a large crate.

Plastic bags

Use clear zipped bags for storing beads or to keep wire in to stop it unraveling. Small sizes are available online.

Microwave bacon trays

These inexpensive ridged trays are ideal for bead sorting and organizing. The ridges allow you to arrange the beads in rows and see what you've got.

Soft table mat

Working on a fabric table mat will protect your work surface from pointed tools such as a cable needle. It will also help to prevent your beads from rolling around, especially if you use one that has got ridges in the weave.

Ruler and tape measure

A tape measure for checking lengths can save a lot of wasted effort. Undoing work is difficult and leaves kinks in the wire, which can cause the wire to break.

Cotton reels and elastic bands

Empty cotton reels are ideal for winding up your hanks of wire (you should never try working straight from the hank as it is guaranteed to knot and tangle). Secure the wrapped wire with an elastic band, then place the cotton reel in a small zipped bag to stop it from unwrapping.

Good light

This is essential to prevent eye strain. It is best to work in daylight, since then you can see the true colors of the beads you are using. Try to look up from your work regularly and refocus on distant objects to give your eyes a rest.

Cotton reels and elastic bands

Basic techniques

KNITTING TECHNIQUES

Making a slip knot

1 Hold the tail of the wire in the left hand, between the thumb and index finger, with the end pointing downward.

2 Tuck the little finger out of the way and make a loop round the first two fingers. Bring the wire back up to the thumb, tucking it under the thumb to hold it in place.

3 Still holding the wire with the thumb and index finger, slide the first and second fingers out of the loop.

4 With the fingers of the right hand, catch the working end of the wire then pull it through the loop.

5 Keep hold of the caught loop, and bring the working wire and the tail together, allowing the loop to slide up the wire and reduce in size.

6 By pulling the working wire, the loop will get smaller, ready to put on either your hook, pin, or needle.

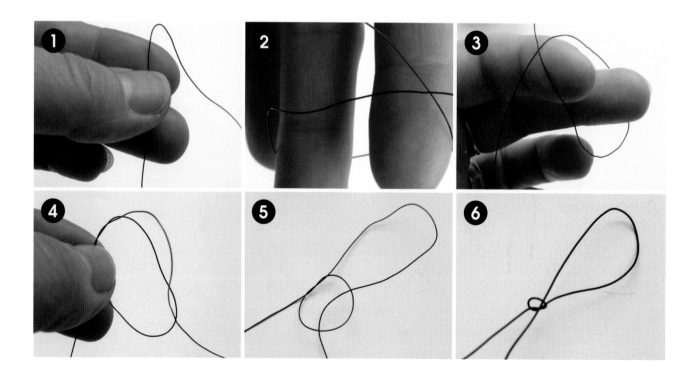

Technique tip...

Keep the wire smooth as you make the slip knot. If you do get a kink in the wire then start again otherwise the loop won't be able to move easily.

Casting on

1 Make a slip knot, and place on the left-hand needle.

2 Insert the right-hand needle into the bottom of the stitch. Then pass the working wire over the point of the right-hand needle from left to right.

3 Draw the loop on the right needle through the first stitch, then make it longer.

4 Put the stitch formed on the right needle onto the left-hand one, and increase the tension on the working wire slightly.

5 Now repeat the process for the required number of stitches.

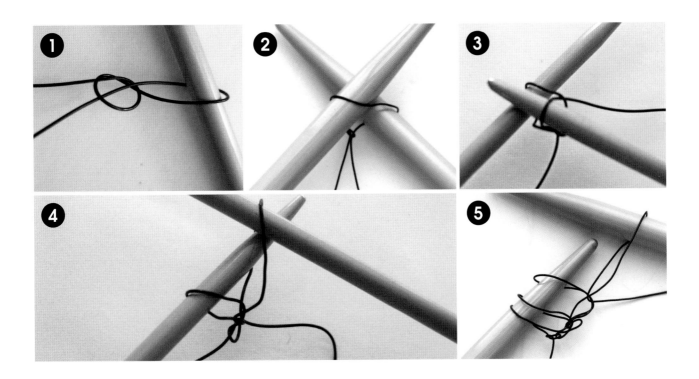

37

Knit stitch

1 Cast on the required number of stitches and hold the needle in your left hand. Insert the right-hand needle into the first stitch as you did when casting on. Wrap the wire over the needle from left to right and draw the loop through.

2 This time, instead of putting the loop back onto the left-hand needle, leave it on the right and slide the loop off the left-hand needle.

3 Continue in this way with the rest of the stitches.

4 When all the loops are on the right-hand needle, put it into your left hand and start again.

> *Technique tip...*
>
> *All of the knitting projects in this book use this simple stitch. Other stitch types are not necessary as the texture you get with them becomes lost when working with wire.*

Beading in knitting

This is how to place a large bead in the center of your work. This example uses eight stitches.

1 Work until you are ready to place your bead and then bring a bead up the wire.

2 Beading row 1: Knit 2, Slip 4.

3 Knit 1 st with the bead, to place it in position, then Knit 1.

4 Beading row 2: Knit 2, Knit 4 into the back of the stitch (this is easier than trying to knit into the front of the stitch). Knit 2.

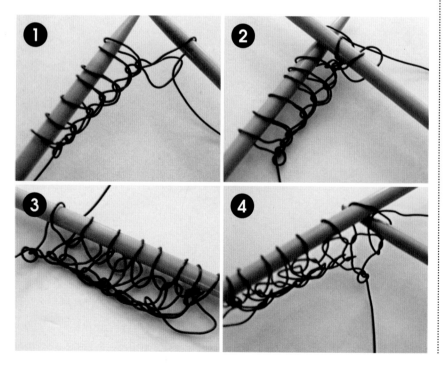

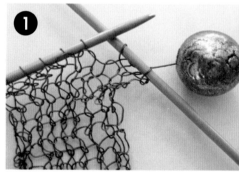

Technique tip…

Notice the loop of wire that keeps the bead in place when you knit a large bead, see picture 3 below. Try to keep this quite tight when working the beading stitch. If you want to make this smaller, then you can slip stitch fewer stitches, but the bead may then sit "proud" of the work.

Beading across a row

1 Bring a bead up the wire ready to place in your work.

2 Knit the first stitch, and then place the bead.

3 Judge whether you can bead on every stitch or on alternate stitches; this depends on the size of the bead. Here the beads are placed on alternate stitches.

4 Make sure that you give the beads enough space to sit well on your work.

Technique tip…

Always bead on the same side of the work— the one that faces away from you when knitting or crocheting. It is important not to use really heavy beads as they will sag and not be supported by the wire.

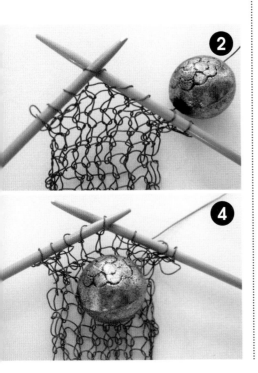

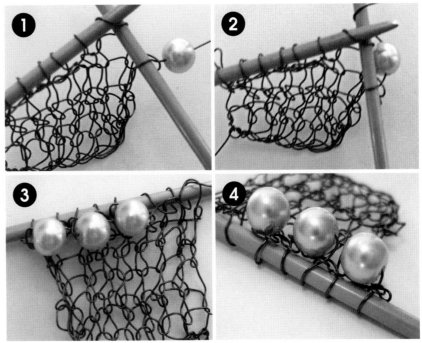

Binding off

1 Knit the required length and then the first 2 sts of the next row. Insert the left-hand needle into the first st on the right-hand needle.

2 Pass the first st over the second st and drop it off the needle, leaving 1 st remaining.

3 Knit 1 st from the left-hand needle, and then repeat the process for the required number of sts.

4 When only 1 st remains on the right-hand needle, cut the working end of wire at about 4in (10cm). Pass it through the remaining st, pulling it gently to reduce the size of the last st.

Technique tip...

All the projects in this book use the conventional method of binding off used in knitting. You could simply pass the working end of the wire through the loops to secure them. However, this tends to gather up the work, which may not be the effect you want to create.

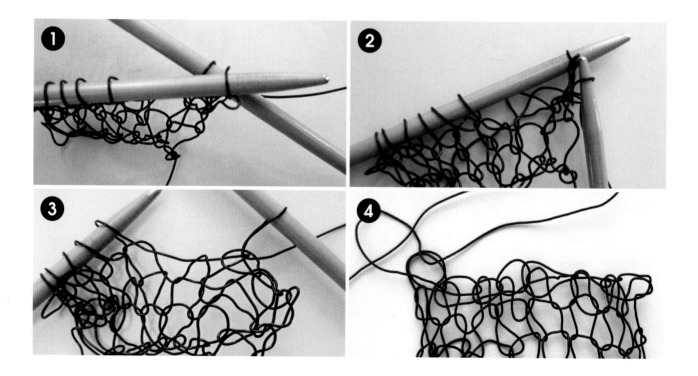

CROCHET TECHNIQUES

Crochet chain stitch

1 Make a slip knot (see page 36 for instructions).

2 Insert the hook into the loop and tighten slightly.

3 Holding the hook between the thumb and the index finger, and the tail in the left hand, pass the working wire over the top of the hook and under, forming a loop.

4 With the head of the hook turned to the left, pass it through the loop on the hook, catching the loop formed as you go.

5 Repeat from step 3, keeping even tension on the wire. To finish off your work, pass the working end of the wire through the final loop of your work, and pull gently.

> *Technique tip...*
>
> *The best way to get good results with crochet is to try to keep your tension even; do not be tempted to pull the loops tightly as you work them. It is worth working a few chains with some scrap wire before you start a project if crochet is new to you.*

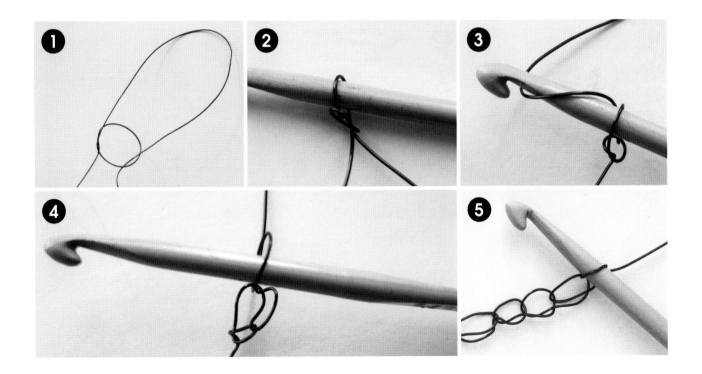

Basic techniques

Slip stitch or single crochet

1 Work as for chain stitch but before passing the working wire over the hook, insert the hook into the work. This puts a second loop on the hook.

2 Pass the wire over the end of the hook, and draw the hook through both loops on the hook.

3 Repeat, taking care not to pull the work too tightly. Finish by passing the working wire through the final loop.

Technique tip...

This is basically the same action as chain stitch. It is used for joining stitches or adding substance to your work. This stitch makes a close, neat join in the work but you do need to leave enough space to insert the hook into the work.

Double crochet (UK: treble crochet)

1 Start with a loop on the hook. Pass the wire over the hook.

2 Insert the hook into the work (there will be three loops on the hook).

3 Pass the wire over the hook again and draw it through the first loop on the crochet hook (three loops on hook).

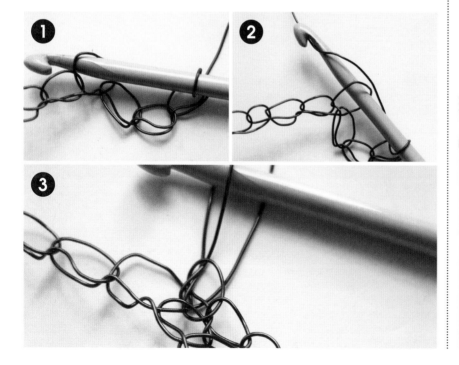

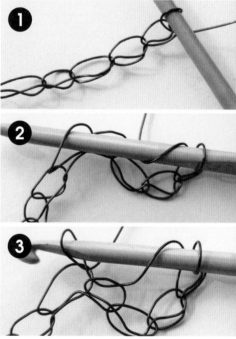

4 Pass the wire over the hook and draw it through the first two loops on the hook (two loops on hook).

5 Pass the wire over the hook and draw it through the remaining two loops.

6 Continue for the required number of sts, then finish off by passing the working wire through the final loop.

Beading in crochet

1 Thread the required number of beads onto the wire and work several chain.

2 Place a bead into the desired position, then pass the wire over the hook and draw it through the loop.

3 Continue with chain stitch; the bead should sit in the same position on the work.

4 Continue, placing beads where you require. Try to keep the tension even and the stitches a regular size.

Technique tip...

When using double crochet (UK: treble), the bead can be placed midway through the stitch (see Zest on page 98).

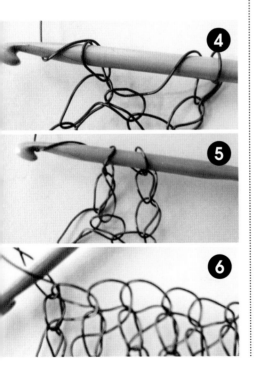

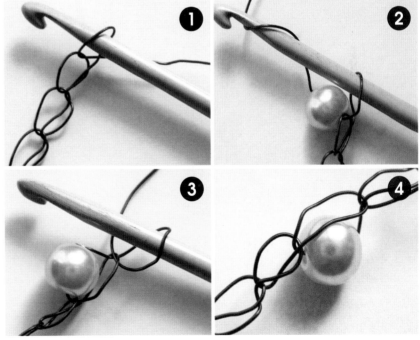

Basic techniques

HOW TO FRENCH KNIT

1 Make a slip knot (see page 36), leaving a long tail of wire.

2 Put the loop over one of the bobbin pins, keeping it fairly loose.

3 Pass the tail of wire down the center of the bobbin.

4 Working clockwise, take the wire across to the far edge of the next pin, around the back and then to the front again, forming a loop of wire around the pin.

5 Continue round the next pins until you are back at the slip knot pin. Work a loop around this pin too.

6 Using a metal point, lift the bottom st over the top one.

7 Continue working in a clockwise direction, 1 st at a time. After each st, give a gentle tug on the wire at the bottom of the bobbin.

8 To finish off, carefully slide the 4 loops off the pins.

9 Pass the working end of the wire through the loops.

10 Pull the working end gently, but firmly, to gather the ends together neatly.

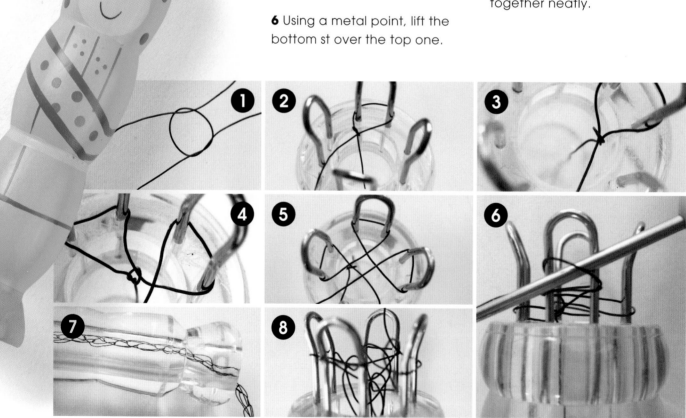

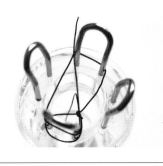
HOW TO PLAIT

1 Secure five strands together at the end and then fix to a secure base. (Use a spare wire to attach them to a drawer handle or similar).

2 Spread the strands out. Begin by crossing the outside right strand over the two strands to its left so it goes to the middle.

3 Cross the left strand over the strands to its right, so it too goes to the middle.

4 Repeat for the length of the strands.

5 The work can be squeezed and teased into shape when you have finished, and before any fastenings are attached.

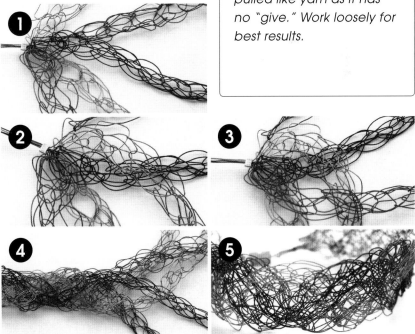

Basic jewelry techniques

ATTACHING FASTENINGS

You can buy many different types of fastening so be sure to choose one that is appropriate to the work. A chunky necklace needs to be matched with a fairly chunky fastening. I prefer fastenings to be discreet, however, you might like to make a statement and use something big and bold at the front of the necklace. Bracelets often have a ring-and-bar type of fastening, for ease of use.

Attaching the fastening

1 Feed two crimp beads onto the finishing wire.

2 Select the fastening of your choice, and check that the ring is closed on the fastening. Squeeze gently with some pliers to secure.

3 Pass the finishing wires through the loop and then back through both of the crimp beads.

Ring-and-bar clasps

Lobster clasps

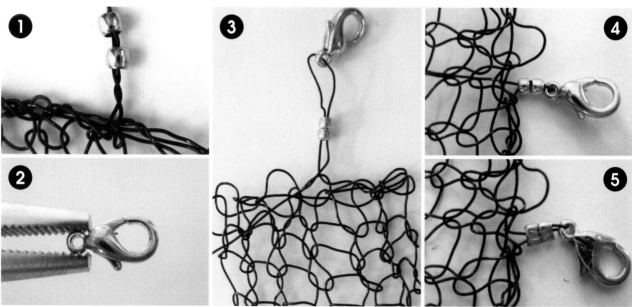

4 Gently pull the wire tails to close the wire loop.

5 Squeeze the crimp beads with pliers and snip off the wire ends.

6 Check that the wire ends are not sticking out. Then, if necessary, bend them back on themselves with the pliers.

7 Repeat for the other half of the fastening. Here, you can see a barrel-type fastening.

Making a fastening loop

Sometimes it is useful to make your own loops for fastening.

1 Twist the finishing wire and feed two crimp beads onto it.

2 Push the twisted wire back down the crimp beads.

3 Adjust the size and squeeze the crimp beads with pliers to secure in place.

4 Finish off the tail.

Crimp beads

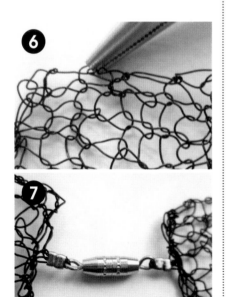

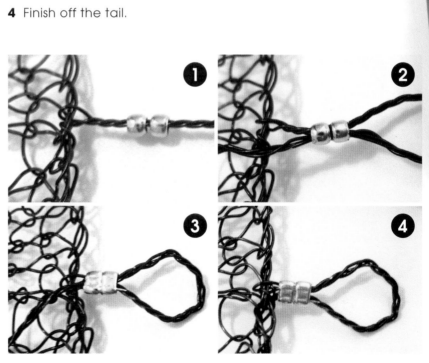

Basic jewelry techniques

Fastenings for chokers

Narrow ribbon—⅛in (4mm)—works well for fastening a choker. You'll need four beads with a reasonable-sized hole that you can fit the ribbon through. You will need four times the desired finished length of ribbon.

1 Finish off the wire ends of the choker.

2 Cut the ribbon in half. Take one piece, fold it in half, and then feed the fold through the center of the finished edge. Pass the two loose ends through the fold to secure.

3 Take a thin piece of wire, fold it in half, and then pass the folded end through the hole in the bead.

4 Taper the ends of the ribbon to a narrow point, using some sharp scissors.

5 Push the pointed end of your ribbon into the fold of the wire.

6 Use the wire to pull the ribbon through the bead.

7 Slide the bead up the ribbon slightly to be able to tie a knot at the end and trim off the end of the ribbon. Slide the bead back down.

8 Repeat for the others.

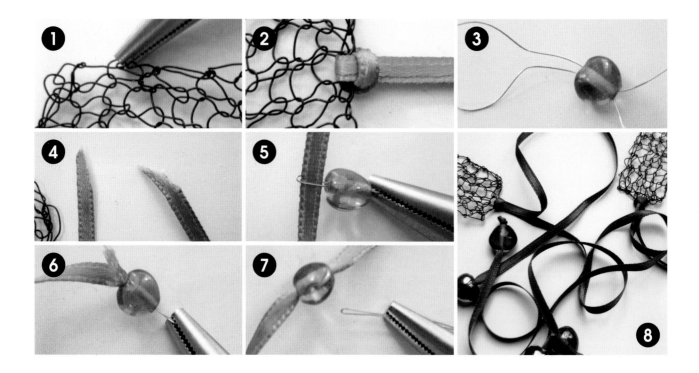

MAKING BRACELETS AND EARRINGS

Bracelets

To make a bracelet to match the necklaces in this book, simply make a shorter version. Measure the length you require round your wrist, remembering that if it is too tight it will be difficult to fasten up. Some bracelets will not require a fastening at all, and can simply be wrapped around the wrist a few times.

Fastenings for bracelets

Larger round or lobster fastenings can be used for bracelets. Alternatively, you can use a ring and bar—if using this type of fastener, the bracelet will need to be shorter. A twist fastening is suitable only for lighter-weight bracelets. Magnetic clasps are best avoided as you can easily lose your bracelet.

Earrings

Earrings can also be made in the same way as the necklace, but are shorter. Their size will depend on your personal taste and the weight of earrings you prefer. Many can be narrower versions of the necklace, which are lighter to wear.

For pierced ears, two types of finding are available: a post type or the shepherd's crook style. Don't forget the backs for the post type, which are often sold separately. If you prefer the clip style, choose this carefully as some are only suitable for sticking on a stone and don't have a loop to attach the earring.

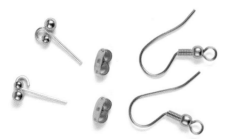

Attaching a fastening to an earring

1 Feed two crimp beads onto the finishing wire.

2 Ensure that the earring loop is fully closed.

3 Pass the finishing wire through the loop and the 2 crimp beads.

4 Gently pull the finishing wire so that the crimp beads are next to the earring.

5 Crimp and cut off the wire as close as possible to the crimps. Make sure there are no ends sticking out.

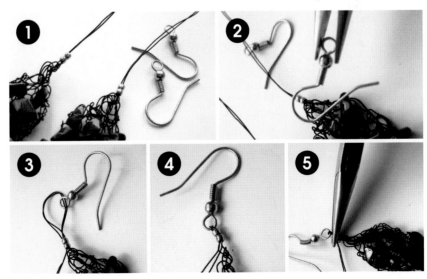

Basic jewelry techniques

Trouble shooting

Snapped wire in the middle of the work

1 Undo a little of the work to give you a "tail" to work with.

2 Take a matching reel of wire and thread any beads from the old reel onto the new reel. Leave another tail of wire before restarting your work with the new reel. Twist the two tails together slightly to stop them slipping and then continue.

3 Complete the work.

4 Then return to the two tails and weave them into the necklace. Don't weave them together as this can make the work bulky. The idea is to disguise the ends in the work so they don't show. If there are suitable beads, tuck the ends inside and snip off. If not, cut the ends close to the work, and use pliers to fold the end neatly into the work.

Snapped wire at the end of the work

1 Hide the broken piece of wire in your work by folding it around another wire and squeezing with pliers.

2 Use a separate piece of wire to attach the fastenings. The wire should be double thickness. Don't try to use the knitting technique of working with 2 pieces of yarn together. This doesn't work for wire as it slips undone.

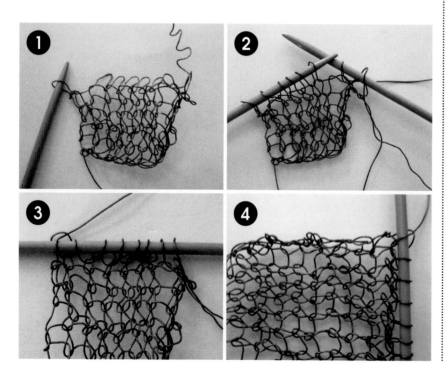

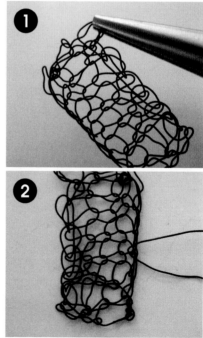

Hiding ends

There are three basic methods for hiding ends. Choose the most appropriate method, remembering to check that there are no uncomfortable wires sticking out.

1 Weave the ends into the work. Weave in opposite directions so the work doesn't become too bulky. Cut and crimp the ends into the work.

2 Tuck the ends inside beads.

3 Feed them through the crimp beads and cut off as close to the crimps as possible.

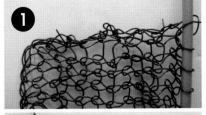

Wire unraveling off the reel

Put the reel inside a small, plastic zipped bag and seal, apart from a small gap through which to feed the wire.

First stitch of French knitting proving difficult

Make the slip loop looser, and you will find that it passes over the hook of the bobbin much more easily.

Finishing off your French knitting

It can be difficult to feed the wire through the bobbin loops while they are still on the bobbin. Slide them off and push a cable needle through the loops to gather together. Feed through the working wire. This should then be easy to pull, tightening the loops.

51

knitting

Confetti

Basic beaded knitting

An easy-to-knit necklace, which can be made with large or small beads. Both produce stunning results. Bracelets and earrings can be made to match.

You will need

65½ft (20m) of 0.315mm (AWG 28:SWG 30) wire

2.25mm (US-1:UK13) short knitting needles

Selection of beads and sequins in various sizes

Crimp beads

Fastening of your choice

For a professional finish…

When arranging your beads, use a tape measure for guidance. Place bigger feature beads every 4in (10cm) and balance your other beads along the length. Play with the colors until you are happy with the result.

Don't bead on each row as you will run out of beads and the necklace will be uncomfortable to wear. Place your beads to fill gaps in the previous row. So, if you place beads on stitches 1, 3, and 5, on the next beading row put them on stitches 2, 4, and 6.

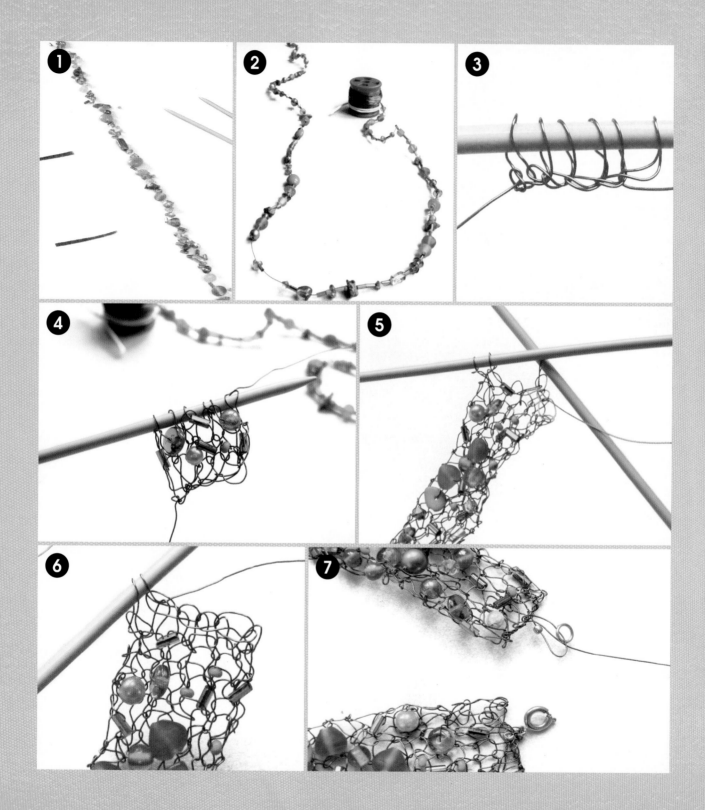

1 Select your beads, and arrange in a line stretching for about 32in (80cm).

2 Unwind about 6ft (2m) of wire from the reel and re-secure with the elastic band. Thread on your beads, mixing sizes and shapes.

3 Cast on 6 sts, leaving a 4in (10cm) tail.

4 Knit Row 1. Knit Row 2, placing 3 or 4 beads across the row.

5 Repeat, adding beads on the even-numbered rows, until you have the required length of about 20in (50cm).

6 To finish, bind off, leaving a 4in (10cm tail). Place the necklace on a flat surface and ease into a curved shape using the palms of your hands.

7 Wrap the tail along the edge to the center, neatening as you go. Use it to attach one half of the fastening. Slip a crimp bead on the wire before looping it between the fixing of the fastening and the center of the edge. Tuck the end of the wire under the crimp bead and squeeze to secure. Cut off any surplus wire. Repeat for the other end.

Variations you can try...

Try making your necklace wider by casting on eight stitches instead of six, or make it narrower by using only four stitches. You can get quite a different look by beading in the center of the necklace only; alternatively, you could place a few larger beads here, making the rest of the necklace wire-only.

For a fun alternative, make a narrow necklace using pink wire and ⅝in (14mm) buttons (you'll need about 40 of them; place the buttons on every fourth row.

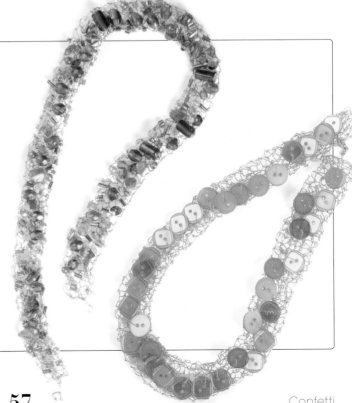

Confetti

Anthracite

Delicate wire collar

A necklace knitted lengthways, making it easy to adjust for length. It has a neat edge, and can readily be made wider or narrower.

You will need

65½ft (20m) of 0.25mm (AWG 30: SWG 33) wire

2.25mm (US-1:UK13) knitting needles

Selection of beads, about ¼in (6mm) in size

Fastening of your choice

For a professional finish…

Casting on needs to be done evenly to get a neat edge. Try to cast on without stopping since the tension will be better this way. The cast on row forms the outside edge of the necklace.

Don't bead on the first or last stitches to ensure that attaching the fastening is easier.

Use beads of ¾in (2cm) or less; any larger and they will hang from the knitting and look unattractive. This is a good project for seed beads or bugle beads.

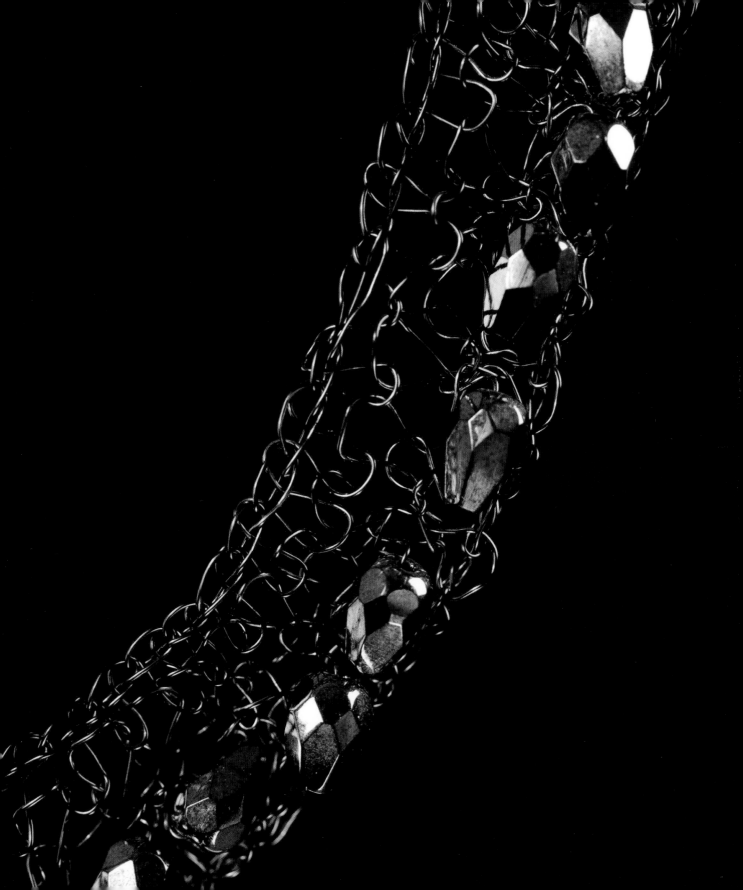

Variations you can try...

Try making the necklace narrower or wider, or add a few central beads. Another variation you could try is random beading—such as having four rows of beads on alternate rows and one central bead.

To make a matching bracelet, cast on 50 sts—this makes a bracelet 8in (20cm) long. Bead in the same way as the necklace. Be sure to bind off evenly and not tightly, and attach the fastening of your choice.

To make earrings, decide on the number of beads you would like and cast on twice this number of stitches plus 3. K2, bead on alternate sts, k2. Bind off and attach fastenings.

1 Thread the beads onto the wire.

2 Cast on 120 sts; 40 sts produces about 6in (15cm) of necklace, so this makes a necklace 18in (46cm) long.

3 Knit 2 rows.

4 Knit 1 st, and bead across this row. Small beads can be on every stitch, larger ones on alternate stitches, as here. The work has been turned over so you can see the beads.

5 Knit 1 row.

6 At the next row, either bind off tightly or repeat from row 4. When binding off, pull the sts quite tightly to make a curve to fit the neck. Try to bind off without stopping as this will give you a more even finish.

7 After binding off, give the whole necklace a gentle tug along its length. Give the outside edge a tug as well, to make it even.

8 Attach the fastenings.

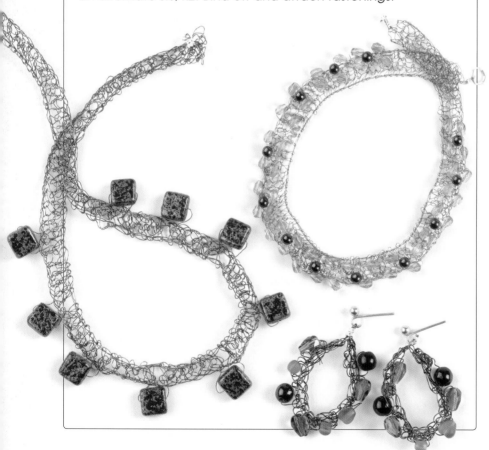

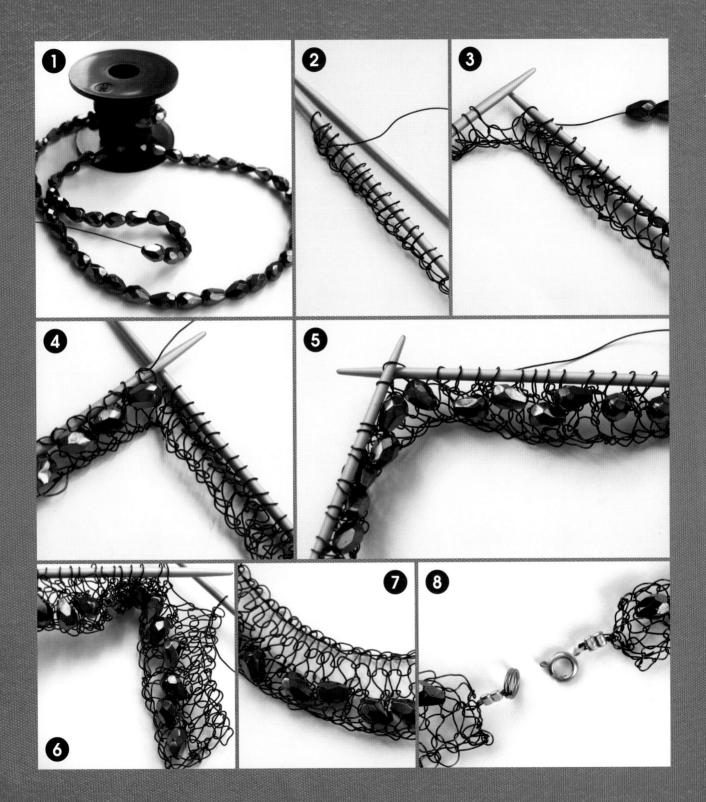

Bauble

Loop-effect wirework

This is a pretty and fragile-looking necklace with a lovely looped edge. Pearl beads give it a classic feel, but the delicate wirework gives it a fresh twist. It is knitted on fine wire, using double-pointed needles.

You will need

65½ft (20m) of 0.25mm (AWG 30, SWG 33) wire

2.25mm (US-1:UK13) double-pointed knitting needles

About 125 beads, approximately ¼in (6mm) in size

Fastening of your choice

For a professional finish…

Be careful not to catch the wire on the bead below as you are beading otherwise you will have a large loop when you've finished. If this does happen, twist the loop into the necklace to hide it.

Work a couple of unbeaded rows at the beginning and end to make attaching the fastening easier.

The loop of wire always falls on the same side of the work. If you are not beading, then this should be the wrong side of the necklace.

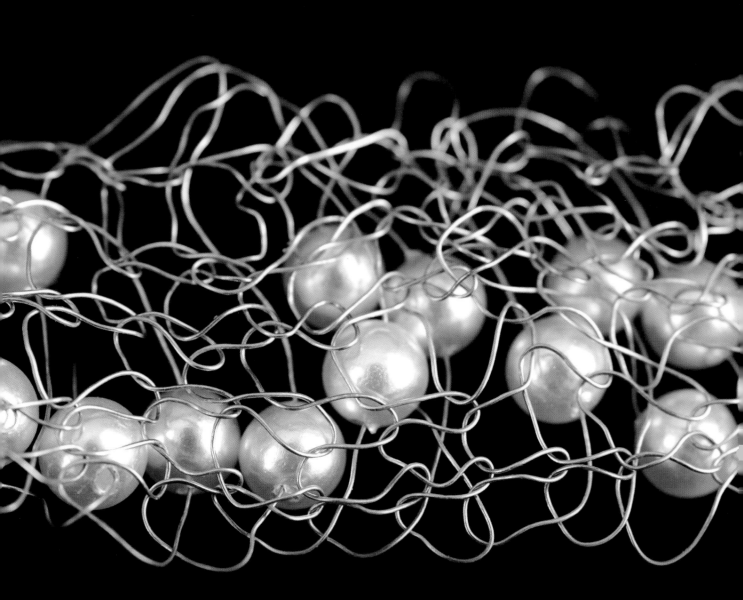

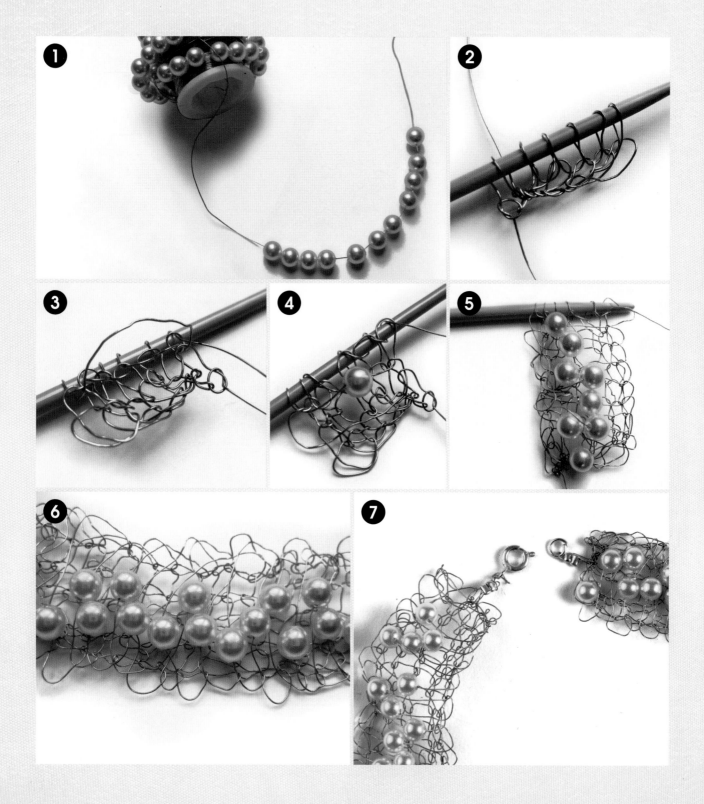

1 Thread the beads on the wire. I used 125 ¼in (6mm) beads to make a necklace 18in (45cm) long.

2 Cast on 6 sts. Then work 1 row. Knit every st—don't slip the first one.

3 Slide the work up to the top of the needle. Work another row. There will be a loop of wire across the work; don't pull this loop tightly across the work as this will stop it from lying flat.

4 Slide the work up to the top of the needle again. Bring up a bead and knit 1 row. (The bead sits on the loop of wire.)

5 Repeat for required length of beading on every row, remembering to slide the work each time. Give a gentle tug after each row to shape the necklace as you go.

6 Bind off with beaded side facing you. When finished, tease out the loops at the edge of the work with one of the needles.

7 Ease the necklace into shape by gently pulling it. Then attach the fastening.

Variations you can try…

This is a very versatile project that works equally well for a narrower necklace (4 sts). It looks good with both random and regular beading, or you can even make an unbeaded version.

Try making the necklace with longer beads, which sit well on the wire. You could also try weaving ⅝in (1.5cm) wide ribbon through the loops—use a large-eyed needle to thread the ribbon through.

For a pair of matching earrings, cast on 3 sts and work four beaded rows. Bind off and attach the posts.

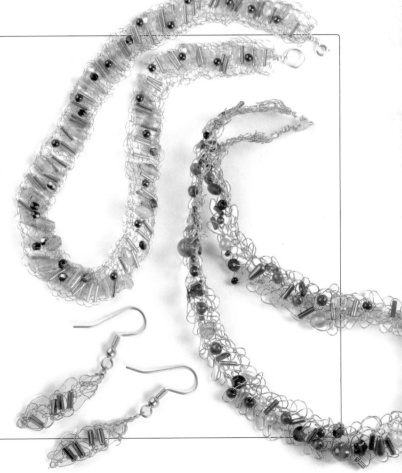

Spiral

Stylish coiled tube

A knitted necklace that looks dramatic and unusual. There is no need to add beads—this necklace makes enough of an impact without them.

You will need

131¼ft (40m) of 0.315mm (AWG 28:SWG 30) wire

2.75mm (US2:UK12) very long knitting needles

10mm (US-15:UK000) chunky knitting needle

Fastening of your choice

For a professional finish...

When wrapping the wire around the knitting needle, wrap at a slight angle so that the wire doesn't overlap. Use both hands to twist the wire firmly.

Take care not to squeeze or squash the necklace. If needed, it can be wrapped around the needle again to correct any lost shape.

If you have used wire that is too fine to hold the shape then simply thread a ribbon or piece of matching wire inside the spiral, and secure when you attach the fastening.

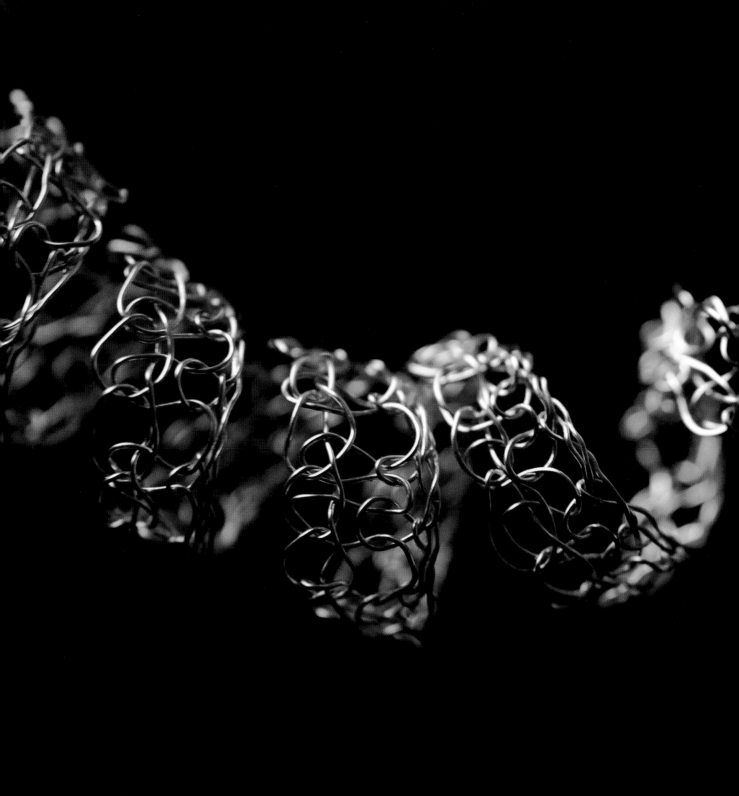

Variations you can try…

For a narrower spiral, wrap the wire around a smaller needle, such as 6.5mm (US-10.5:UK2), and cast on fewer stitches (about 300). You can also try making a narrower spiral inside a wider one, using different colored wire for each.

To make matching earrings, cast on 30 stitches and twist around a 5 or 6mm (US8–10:UK6–4) needle. As a rough guide, the number of stitches you cast on is about twice the finished length of the earring; if you'd like longer earrings, cast on more stitches.

1 Cast on 400 sts.

2 Knit 1 row. Work evenly, not too loosely or tightly. This is the key to getting a good finish.

3 Push the sts up the needle as you work; otherwise you risk losing them off the end. This necklace is hard on your fingers, so be careful.

4 Bind off. As you bind off, give the work a tug to even up the sts.

5 Now, wrap the work tightly around the 10mm (US-15:UK000) knitting needle, flattening it against the needle as you go.

6 When it is all wrapped round the needle, hold the work at each end and twist until you can twist no more. The necklace should stay in place when you let go. Slide it off the needle.

7 Adjust the twists and then attach the fastenings.

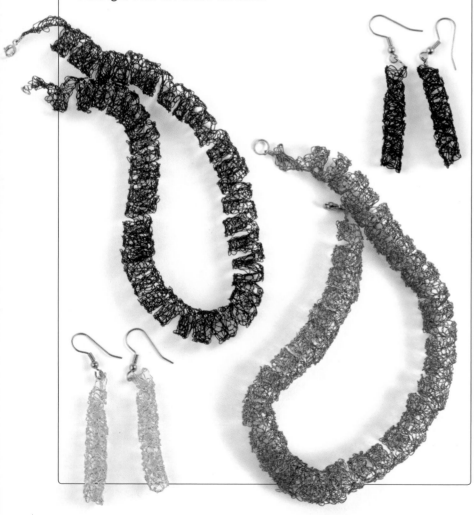

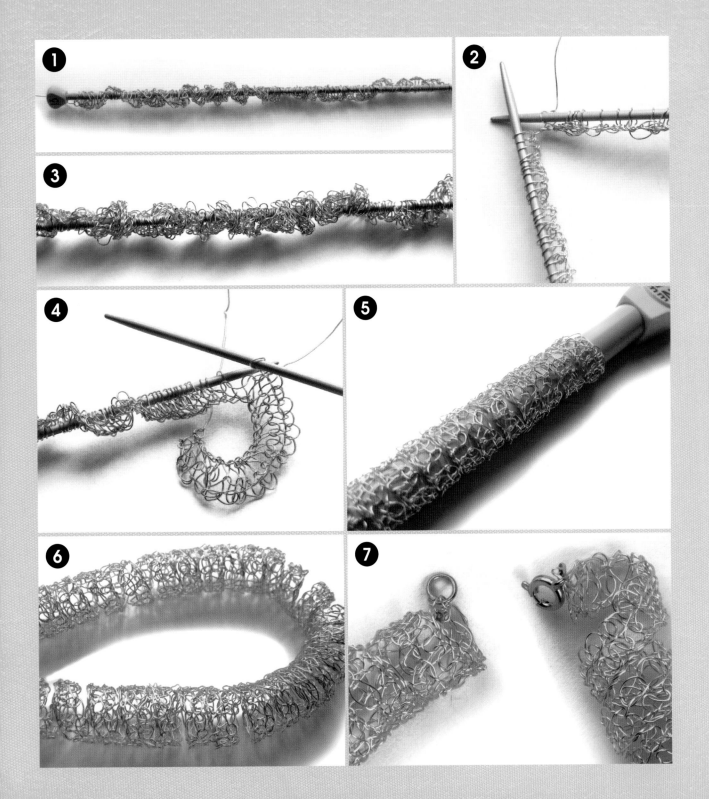

Filigree

Dainty lace stitching

A fragile-looking necklace that looks equally good as a choker or short chain. Enhanced with tiny Swarovski beads that sparkle beautifully, this pretty necklace is a winner for the evening.

You will need

65½ft (20m) of 0.2mm (AWG 32, SWG 36) wire

2.25mm (US-1:UK13) short knitting needles

About 50 Swarovski beads

Magnetic or screw fastening

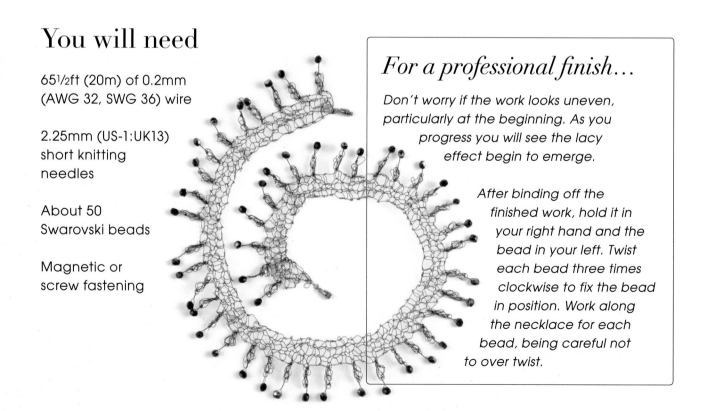

For a professional finish…

Don't worry if the work looks uneven, particularly at the beginning. As you progress you will see the lacy effect begin to emerge.

After binding off the finished work, hold it in your right hand and the bead in your left. Twist each bead three times clockwise to fix the bead in position. Work along the necklace for each bead, being careful not to over twist.

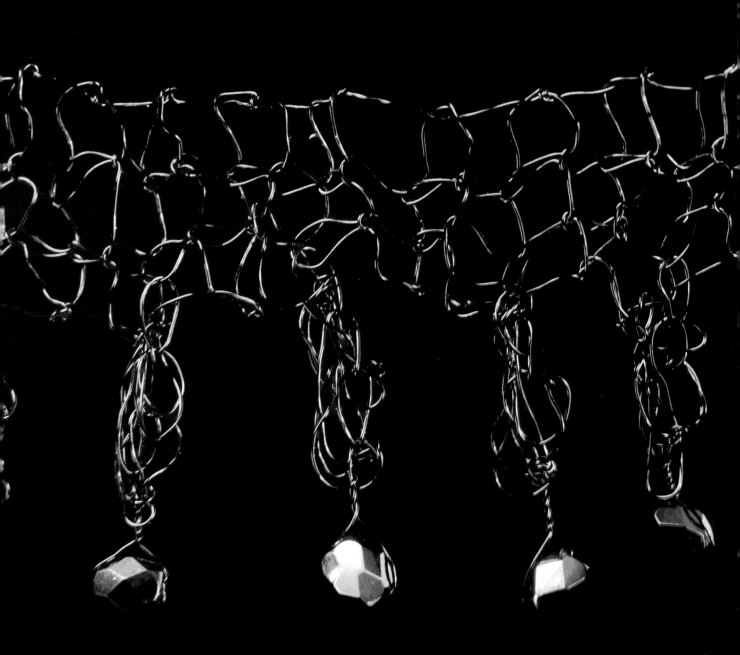

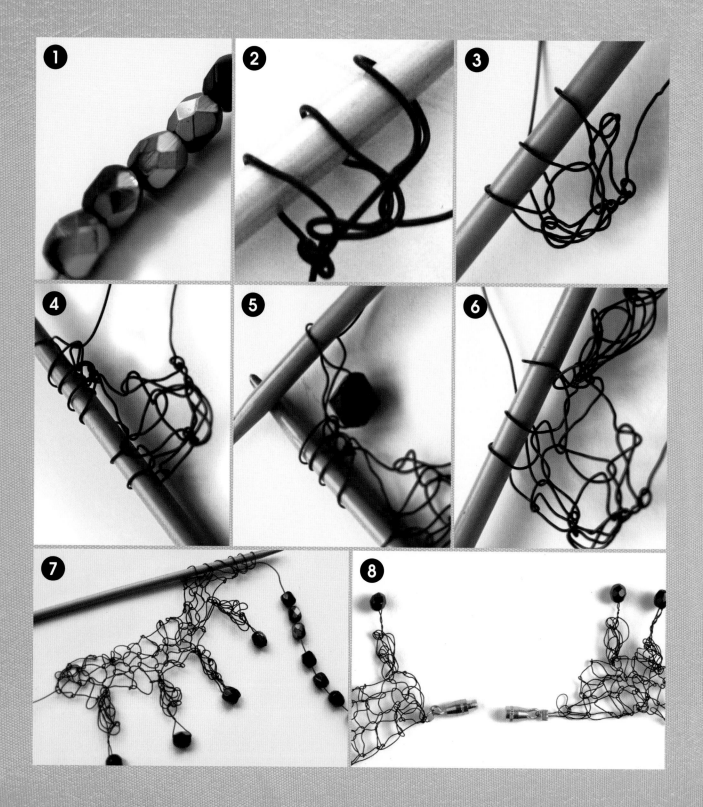

1 Thread the beads onto the wire. The fine wire used means this necklace is quite light.

2 Cast on 3 sts.

3 Knit 3 rows. Work evenly—if you work too tightly, you won't get the delicate effect.

4 Row 4: Cast on 4 sts (7 sts).

5 Row 5: Bead on the first st.

6 Bind off 4 sts and knit the remaining 3 sts. Give the bead a tug as you bind off each stitch to keep them even.

7 Knit 3 rows. Repeat from step 4 until you reach the required length.

8 Work 2 rows, then bind off. Attach the fastening. Use a magnetic or screw fastening, which is easy to secure.

Variations you can try…

It's easy to make a wider or narrower collar by casting on more or fewer stitches at the start.

Earrings can be fun. To make short earrings, cast on 12 stitches, bead, bind off six stitches. Cast on six stitches, bead, then bind off. Alternatively, try casting on and binding off, randomly beading as you please. Make the strands at the top slightly longer so you get more of a "branch" effect. The wire is light so these earrings won't be heavy to wear.

73

French
knitting

Carbon

Basic beaded French knitting

Using this wonderful traditional toy, you can produce an easy and unusual necklace that is different every time you do it. It is also readily adjusted for length.

You will need

65½ft (20m) of 0.315mm (AWG 28, SWG 30) wire

Four-pin French-knitting bobbin

Cable needle

About 70 assorted small beads

Fastening of your choice

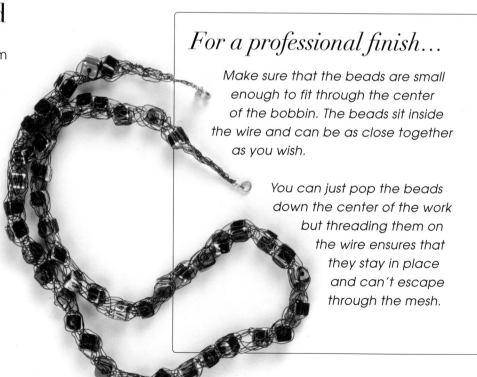

For a professional finish…

Make sure that the beads are small enough to fit through the center of the bobbin. The beads sit inside the wire and can be as close together as you wish.

You can just pop the beads down the center of the work but threading them on the wire ensures that they stay in place and can't escape through the mesh.

1 Thread the beads onto the wire. Make a slip knot and put the loop over one of the bobbin pins.

2 Pass the tail down the center of the bobbin so that it can be pulled from the bottom. This will help tension the work.

3 Start knitting and work 1 complete round. The first st can be difficult to lift over; keep the slip knot loose to make this easier.

4 Work 2 more complete rounds, working in a clockwise direction.

5 Thread the first bead, holding it down the center of the bobbin.

6 Continue knitting until you have the length you want, placing the beads as required.

7 Finish off by sliding the 4 loops off the pins, and passing the working end of the wire through the loops. Pull the working end firmly to gather the ends together.

8 Attach the fastening.

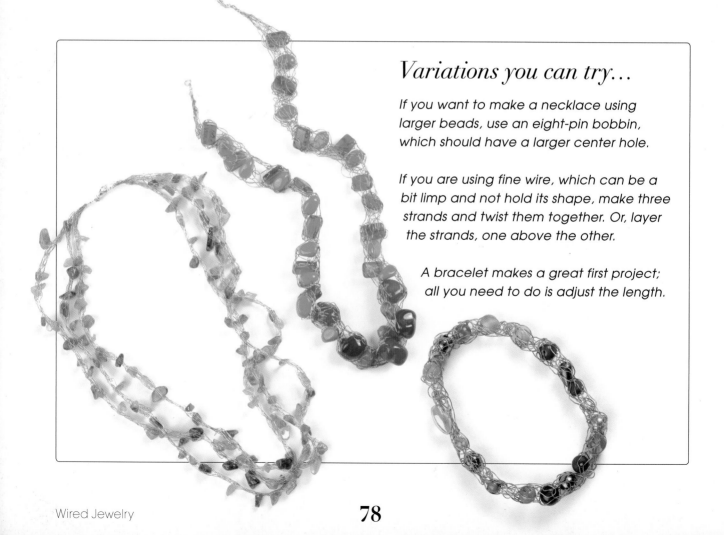

Variations you can try...

If you want to make a necklace using larger beads, use an eight-pin bobbin, which should have a larger center hole.

If you are using fine wire, which can be a bit limp and not hold its shape, make three strands and twist them together. Or, layer the strands, one above the other.

A bracelet makes a great first project; all you need to do is adjust the length.

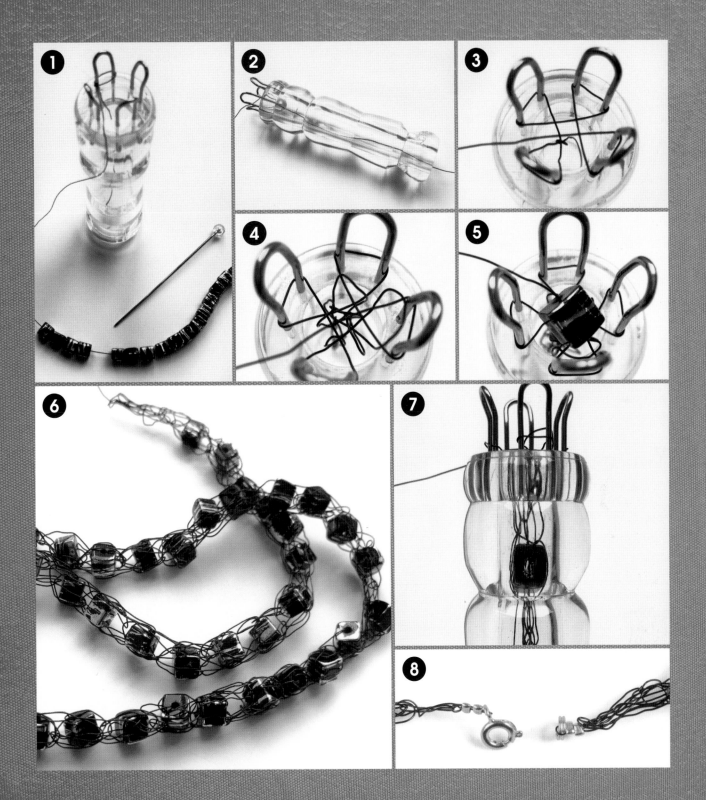

Gossamer

Plain plaited chain

A beautiful, delicate necklace that is easy to adjust
for length and can be worked in a variety of colors
to match any outfit. It is very attractive unbeaded,
or you can add sparkly Swarovski beads.

You will need

65½ft (20m) of 0.2mm
(AWG 32: SWG 36) wire,
3 lengths in 3 toning
colors

Four-pin French-knitting
bobbin

Cable needle

Fastening of your choice

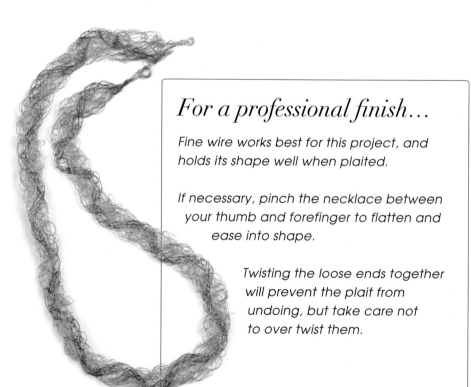

For a professional finish…

*Fine wire works best for this project, and
holds its shape well when plaited.*

*If necessary, pinch the necklace between
your thumb and forefinger to flatten and
ease into shape.*

*Twisting the loose ends together
will prevent the plait from
undoing, but take care not
to over twist them.*

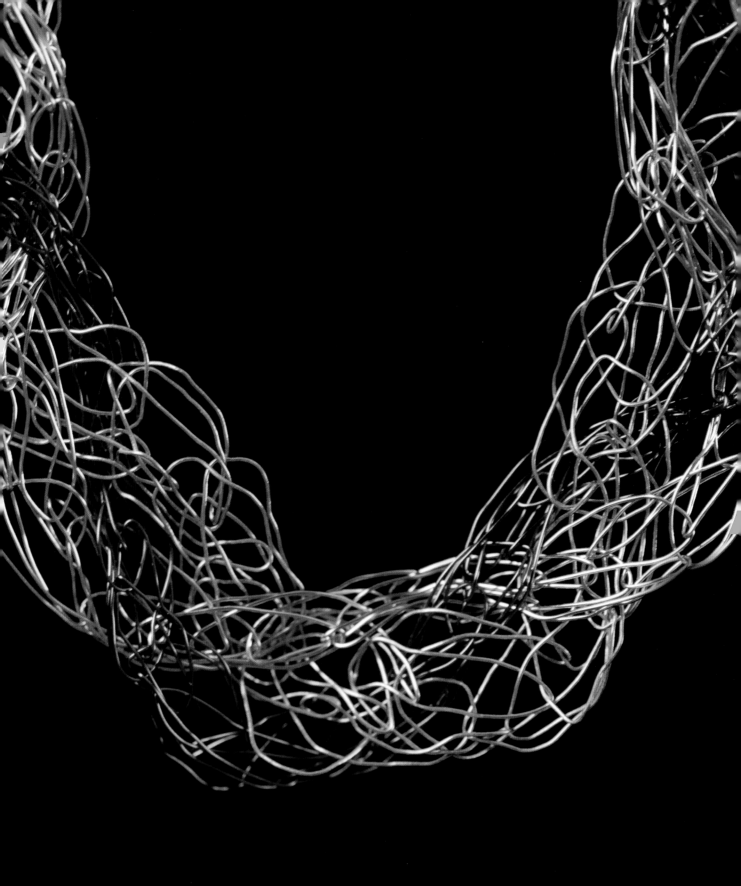

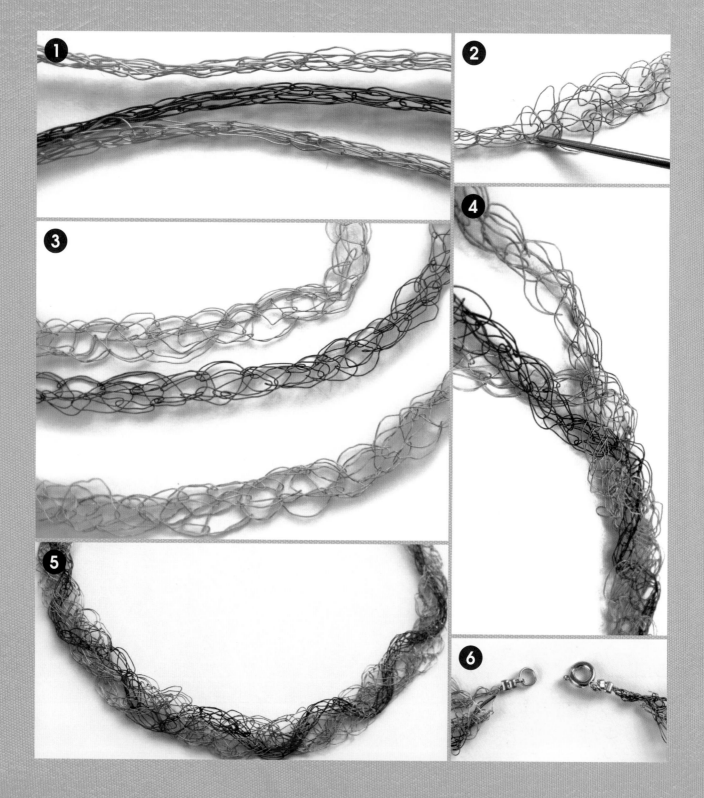

1 Cast on 4 loops, and then work the required length of necklace plus 4in (10cm). Finish off the end. Do this 3 times, using wire of the same weight.

2 The wire will appear rather thin because you will have tugged it through the bobbin as you worked. To rectify this, take each chain in turn, hold it between your thumbs and index fingers, and gently pull it to make it wider. Alternatively, use a cable needle to tease the chain apart.

3 You should find that the chain flattens and makes a band about ½in (1cm) wide. Repeat for all 3.

4 Now twist the 3 ends together. Plait the strands, easing them into shape as you go. Don't pull tightly or the shape of the necklace will distort.

5 Shape on a flat surface when the plaiting is finished and twist the ends together.

6 Attach the fastening.

Variations you can try…

You can use a medium wire, for a firmer, more defined necklace or a choker. Try making two of the three plaits the same color. Or be ambitious and make a five-strand plait.

For a beaded necklace, choose small sparkly beads and a piece of matching wire. Attach the end of the wire close to the fastening and weave it through the plaited work for about ¼in (6mm). Add a bead and continue weaving, making sure that the beads sit on the surface of the necklace. Locate the beads as frequently as you wish, making sure that the weaving wire is hidden well in the plait.

Bracelets and earrings are easy to make, using shorter plaits. Be sure that you don't make the earrings too wide when you are teasing them into shape.

Gossamer

Clementine

Pretty ribbon-weave

An unusual necklace that is worked on two pins for a delicate and light effect. Weaving a fine ribbon through the wire finishes off your necklace—adding a large central bead gives it a different dimension altogether.

You will need

65½ft (20m) of 0.315 (AWG 28, SWG 30) wire

Four-pin French-knitting bobbin

Cable needle

Length of ribbon of desired length

Selection of beads, if required

Magnetic or twist fastening

For a professional finish…

The chain will be narrow at first because you will have tugged it through the bobbin. Tease it out carefully. You can use your fingers, but it might make them feel a bit sore; you may prefer to use the point of a cable needle instead.

Make sure there are no sharp ends of wire to scratch the skin. Bend them carefully back into the work with pliers.

1 Make a slip knot, put the loop over one of the bobbin pins, and pass the tail down the center of the bobbin.

2 Work on 2 opposite pins to make a chain.

3 Continue working until the chain is 1¼in (3cm) longer than the finished length that you require.

4 Finish off the loops, and remove from the bobbin.

5 On a soft surface—such as a fabric table mat—tease out the wire into a looped, open chain.

6 Using the point of the cable needle, thread a ribbon through the center of the wire, keeping it as flat as possible.

7 Before you attach a fastening, the end of the ribbon needs to be secured. Taper the end of the ribbon, and pass it through a larger crimp bead before threading through the wire. Trim the ribbon off close to the first crimp bead. Attach the fastenings.

8 Attach the beads after you have finished making the necklace. As this necklace is lightweight, the beads should be, too. Use a separate piece of wire and weave the end through the work, bead one at a time. Try to place the beads centrally for best effect.

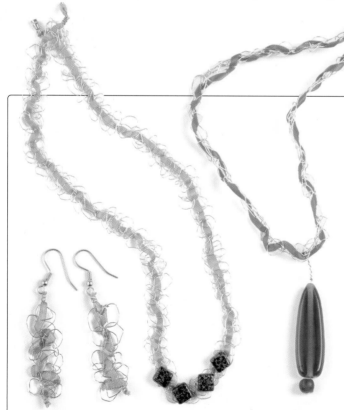

Variations you can try…

Using different colored ribbon and beads will give your necklace a quite different look. You could use two pieces of ribbon of different colors, and perhaps attach a central drop as well. For a lacy effect, try using a lighter wire on a larger bobbin.

Try making earrings to match. Count the rounds very carefully so they both finish up the same length.

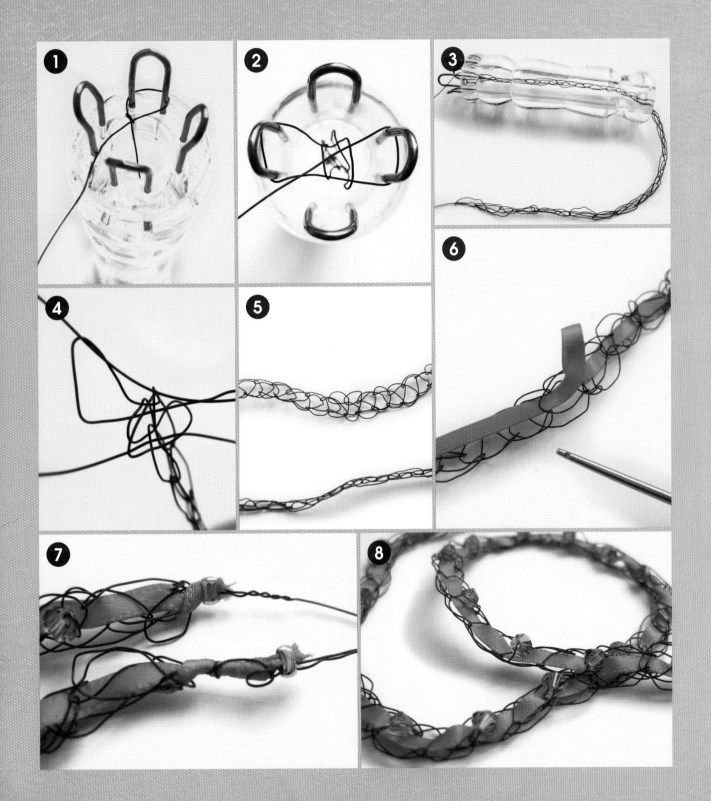

Electric

Two-stranded twisting

This necklace is worked on four pins and twisted back on itself to make a flat, attractive necklace. It uses two strands of wire together, and the subtle colors reflect the light well.

You will need

2 x 65½ft (20m) lengths of 0.2mm (AWG 32, SWG 36) wire, in contrasting colors

Four-pin French-knitting bobbin

Sewing needle

Selection of ¼in (6mm) Swarovski beads

Fastening of your choice

For a professional finish…

When twisting the work together try to keep the twists flat. The beading wire will hold the twists in place and won't show when completed.

Make sure the sewing needle will pass through the hole in the beads. If not, unthread and simply push the wire through the beads. Try not to kink the beading wire as it will make it tricky to pull through the work.

Don't use thicker wire, as it can be difficult to handle when working two strands together.

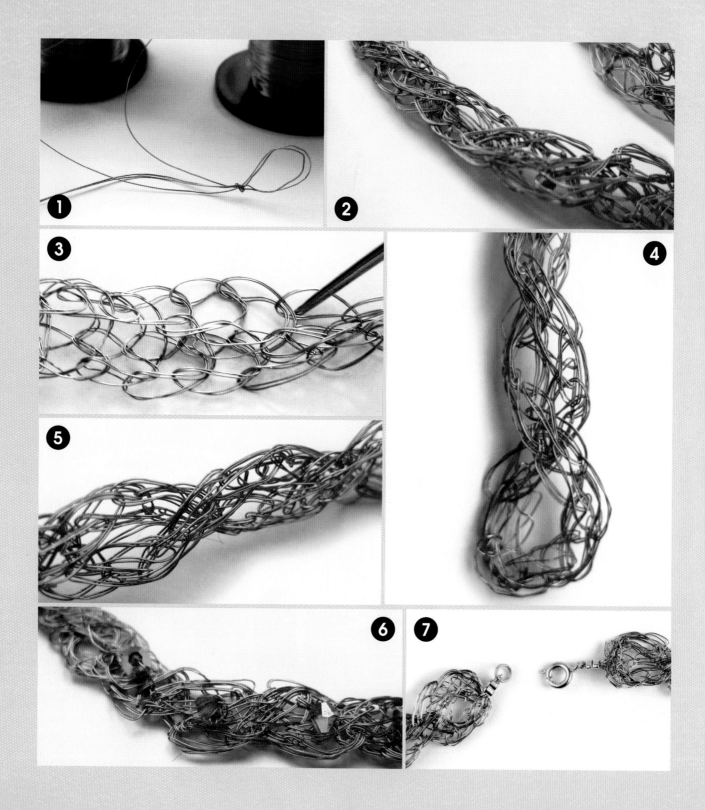

1 Make a slip knot with both pieces of wire together.

2 Work the required length of knitting: this will be twice the finished necklace length plus 4in (10cm), then finish the ends.

3 Tease out the width of the work between the fingers so that it is about ½in (1cm) wide.

4 Fold the knitting in half and begin twisting the two halves together in an "S" pattern. Keep the work even and the twists of a regular size.

5 When you get to the other end, use the loose wire ends to join the 2 pieces together. The knitting is very forgiving and the wire ends won't show when woven in.

6 To add Swarovski beads, use a length of wire and thread it into a sewing needle. Then, beginning at the rounded end, leave a tail of wire and work a running stitch along the necklace's length to where you want to place the beads. Bring the needle to the right side of the work and slip on a bead. Pass the needle down through the work close to where the bead is to sit.

Bring the needle up again next to the bead. Continue working with the running stitch and add the beads, one at a time, where needed.

7 When you reach the end of the necklace, include the beading wire with the twisted ends, then attach the fastenings.

Variations you can try…

Strong contrasts are very effective, but you could use toning colors instead—for example, gold and brown—to create a more subtle effect. Avoid using colors that are too similar as they will blend into each other too much. A single-color necklace, on the other hand, can look quite dramatic.

If you would like a wider necklace, then use a bobbin that has eight pins. The thicker width would work well for a matching bracelet.

Earrings need about 4in (10cm) of plait to be twisted satisfactorily. Work exactly as for the necklace and attach suitable findings.

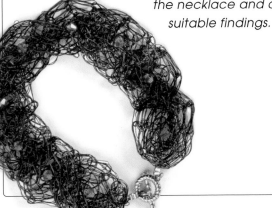

Electric

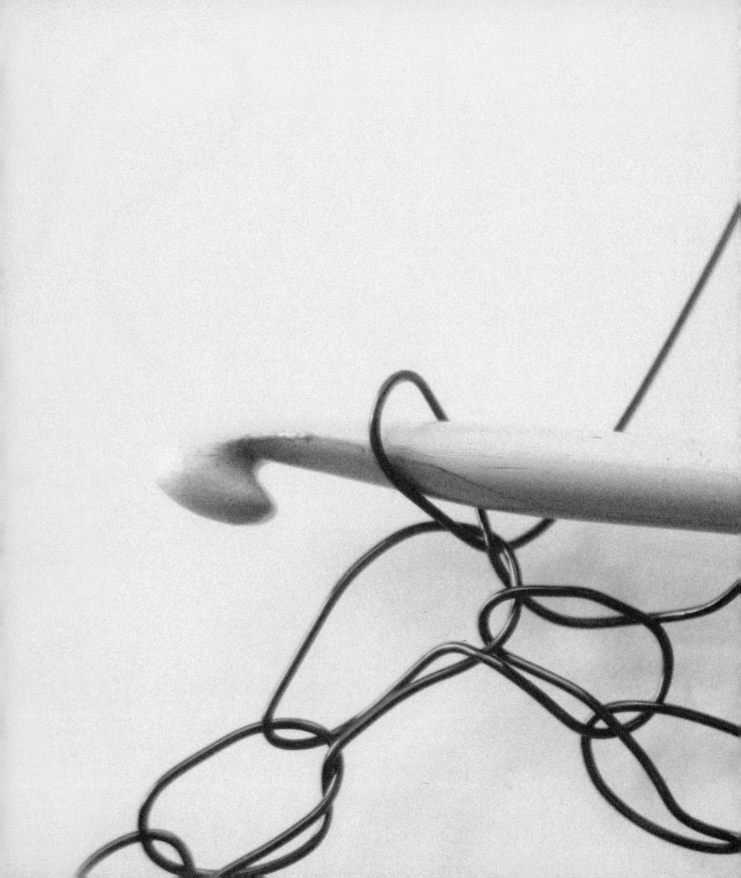

crochet

Cobalt

Basic beaded crochet

This is a simple crocheted necklace that can easily
be adjusted for a variety of lengths. It can also be made
up of single or multiple strands.

You will need

65½ft (20m) of 0.25mm
(AWG 30:SWG 33) wire

2.75mm
(USC2:UK12)
crochet hook

Selection of
beads

Fastening of
your choice

For a professional finish…

*Try working a few chain stitches
on a scrap piece of wire to practise
getting the perfect tension. Don't
pull the wire too tightly.*

*It is better to work this necklace in one
sitting as the tension will be more even
and the beads will sit better on
the chain.*

*Try not to work more chain
than is needed; the wire is
likely to snap if you try to undo
your stitches, and the kinks are
difficult to remove.*

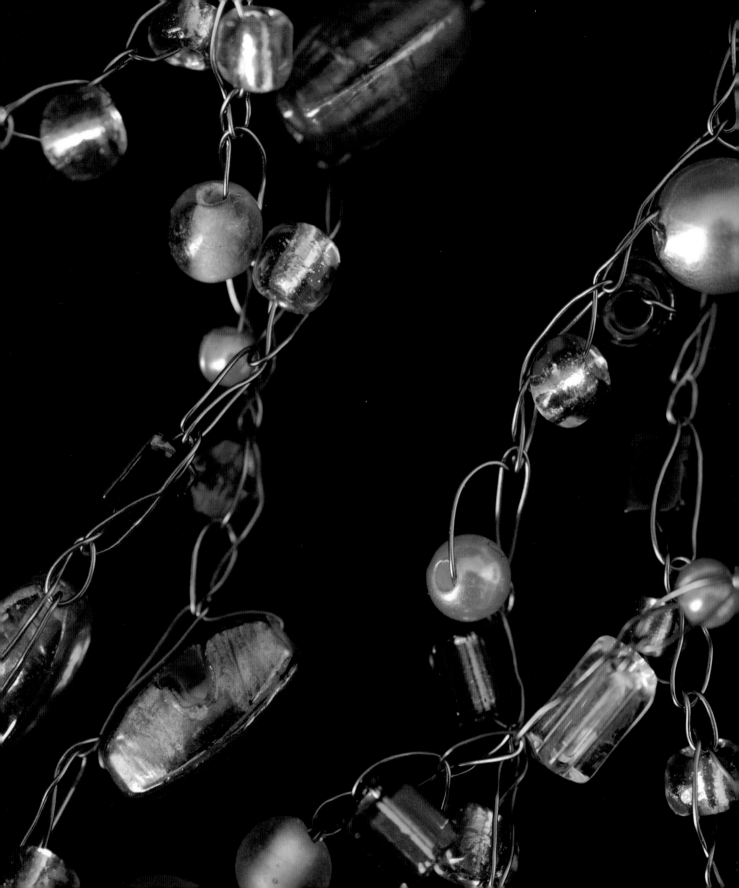

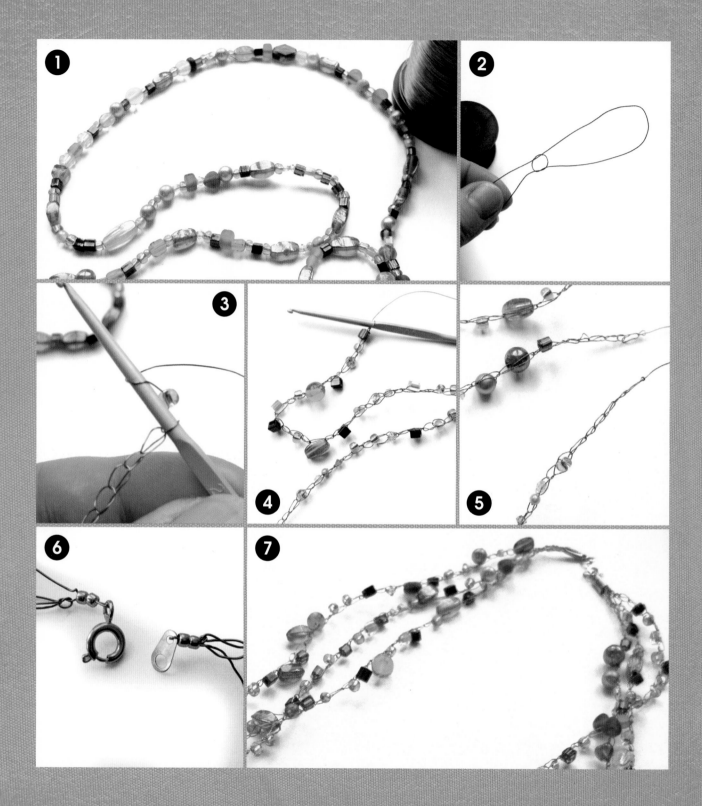

1. Unwind about 6ft (2m) of wire and thread on your beads. Secure the remaining wire onto the reel with an elastic band.

2. Make a slip knot in the wire.

3. Begin crocheting and work about 6 chain.

4. Bead on alternate chain sts until you reach the required length; about 27in (70cm) is a good length. If you are using larger beads, place them further apart.

5. Finish with 6 chain to match the beginning.

6. Cut the wire and pass it through the last chain to secure. Attach a fastening if you are making a single chain.

7. If you want to make a necklace with several strands, repeat the process two or three times more, making each chain shorter by 3in (7cm). Lay the strands out flat and ease out any kinks. Bring the ends together and pass through 1 crimp bead. Adjust and squeeze crimp to hold the ends; this makes attaching a fastening much easier to do.

Variations to try…

Work more than one chain in different colors, adjusting the length of strands so that they sit nicely on your neck. Place heavier beads at the center of the necklace for a more dramatic effect, or add a feature bead at the center. You could also try randomly placing assorted beads and working several chains. Experiment with hooks; the larger the hook that you use, the "loopier" the chain.

To make a matching bracelet, create a long continuous chain and join it end to end without a fastening. Wrap it around the wrist several times to wear.

For earrings, make a short beaded chain joined in a loop, and attach them to the ear wire with crimp beads.

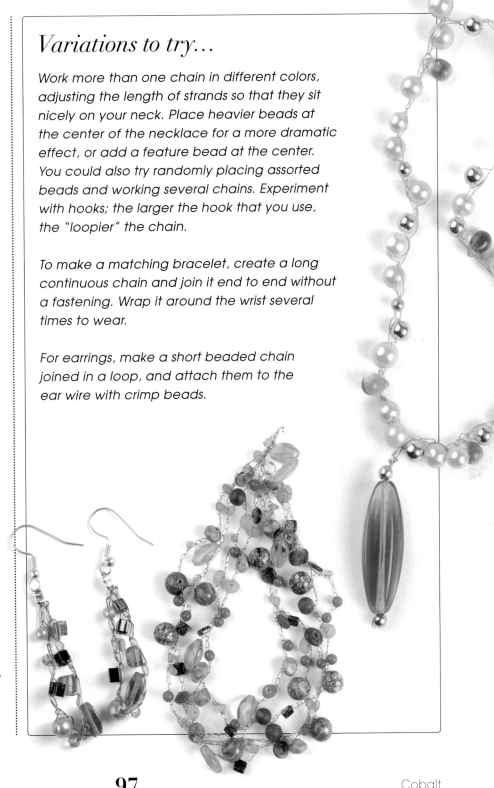

Cobalt

Zest

Pretty chain-stitch collar

A simple crochet collar that can be easily adjusted for length. It works well as a choker, and uses chain stitch and double crochet (UK: treble crochet).

You will need

65½ft (20m) of 0.315mm (AWG 28: SWG 36) wire

2mm (USB-0:UK14) crochet hook

Selection of beads, such as ¼in (6mm) bugle beads

Fastening of your choice

For a professional finish…

Don't be tempted to pull the chain loops too tightly. This will spoil the finished piece, which won't sit properly on the neck.

The weight of wire may seem a little heavy. However, it works well because the design of the necklace is quite "open."

The chain is the inside edge, and you may need to tease the necklace into shape with the thumb and forefinger of each hand. Tug gently, working your way round the necklace. If the beads are not in quite the right place, use the point of a cable needle to move them into shape.

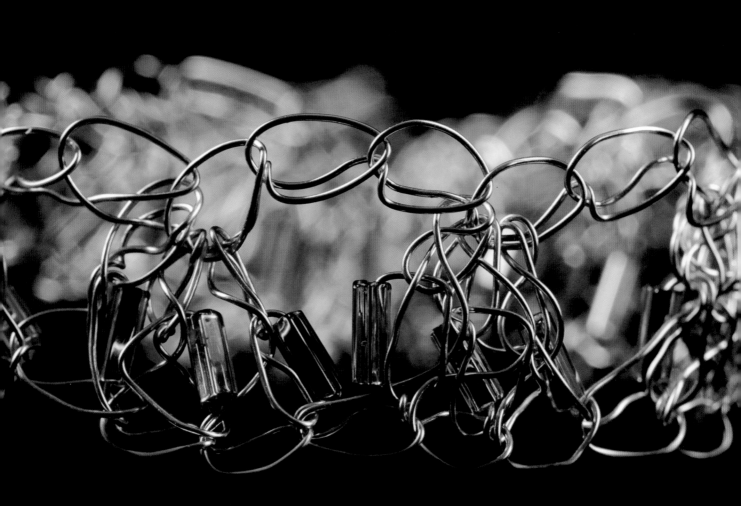

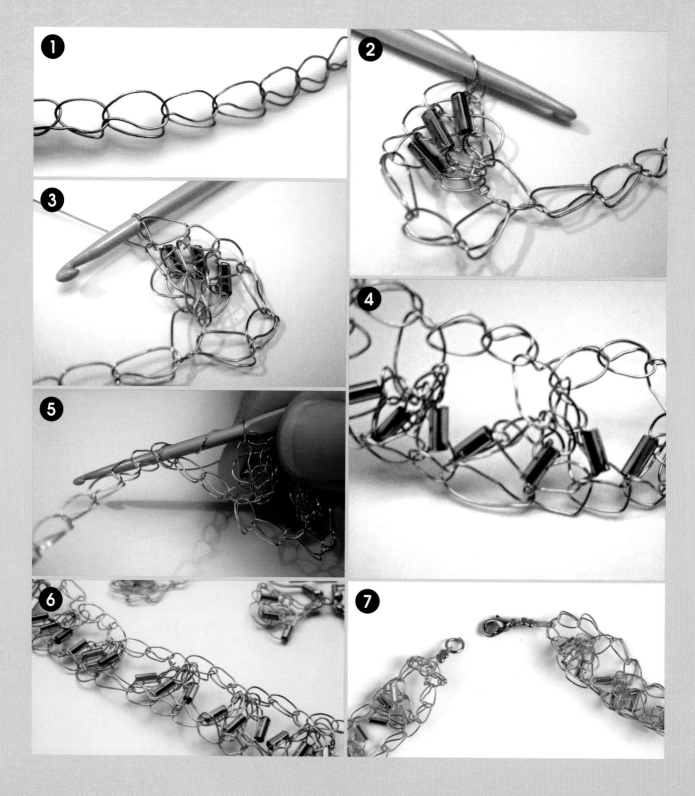

1 Thread the beads, if using, onto the wire. Work an even chain, producing the required length of the necklace plus an extra 5 chain.

2 Turn the work. Work a double crochet (UK: treble) into the fourth chain from the hook but before you do the last part of the stitch, bring up a bead, and then finish the stitch.

3 Work 2 more double crochet (UK: treble) into the same chain, beading as you did on the first stitch.

4 The beads will sit on the wrong side of the work in a fan shape.

5 Miss 2 chain and work the next cluster of double crochet (UK: treble), beading as before.

6 Work the clusters along the length of the chain you made.

7 When you reach the end of the chain, work 1 or 2 double crochet (UK: treble) without beading to complete the necklace. Attach the fastening to finish.

Variations you can try...

Beading can be done on the initial chain, too. Bead on every third loop and make this the loop that you work the double crochet (UK: treble) cluster into. For a very simple and delicate necklace, try making an unbeaded version.

To make matching earrings, put three beads onto the wire. Make a slip loop and work three chain, placing a bead on the last chain. Work two double crochet (UK: treble) into the first chain you made, beading on the last part of the stitch. Finish off, then weave this piece of wire up to the top, and use it to attach the findings.

101

Cluster

Chunky crochet plait

A beautiful chunky necklace, which uses toning beads to good effect on three chains. This method works particularly well for bracelets, too.

You will need

65½ft (20m) of 0.315mm
(AWG 28: SWG 30) wire

3mm (USD-3:UK10) crochet hook

Selection of beads

Fastening of your choice

For a professional finish...

Make the bead mixture really random by putting the beads in a dish and giving them a good stir. Select your beads by dipping into the dish without looking.

The chain needs to be about 28in (70cm) for a finished necklace length of 23in (60cm). Adjust accordingly if you want a shorter necklace.

If the necklace is too long when you have finished, simply scrunch it up. Push the chains together and make a denser necklace.

1 Thread the beads onto the wire (you need plenty of them as you are going to make 3 strands). Make a slip loop, then crochet 2 chain.

2 Bead, crochet 1 chain, bead, crochet 1 chain. Repeat to end.

3 Make the strand the finished necklace length plus 4in (10cm). Finish by passing tail through the last chain loop.

4 Repeat 2 more times. Then take the 3 crochet strands and twist together the ends of wire.

5 Fix the twisted wires to a drawer handle or something secure and begin to plait. Overlap the strands, easing the beads into place so that they sit nicely without gaps. The plait doesn't need to be tight so don't pull too much.

6 Finish the ends by twisting them together, and then attach the fastenings.

Variations you can try...

This is a great necklace for using up any odd beads, and a toning mixture of variously sized beads works really well. Try alternating a gold-colored spacer bead between the colored beads, for an evening necklace, or try smaller beads for a lighter effect.

For an even chunkier necklace, you can make five strands and plait them together. Make a shorter length for a matching bracelet, but be sure to use a secure fastening since this design can be quite heavy.

Azure

Dramatic center drop

An easy-to-make necklace featuring a large central bead to make a dramatic impact. It works equally well for daytime or night-time, depending on the beads that you use. Larger ones are best.

You will need

65½ft (20m) of 0.315mm (AWG 28:SWG 30) wire

3.25mm (USD-3:UK10) crochet hook

Selection of beads

Fastening of your choice

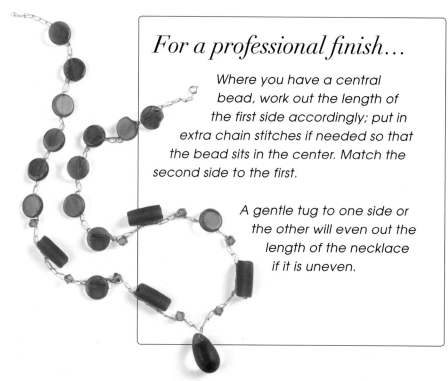

For a professional finish...

Where you have a central bead, work out the length of the first side accordingly; put in extra chain stitches if needed so that the bead sits in the center. Match the second side to the first.

A gentle tug to one side or the other will even out the length of the necklace if it is uneven.

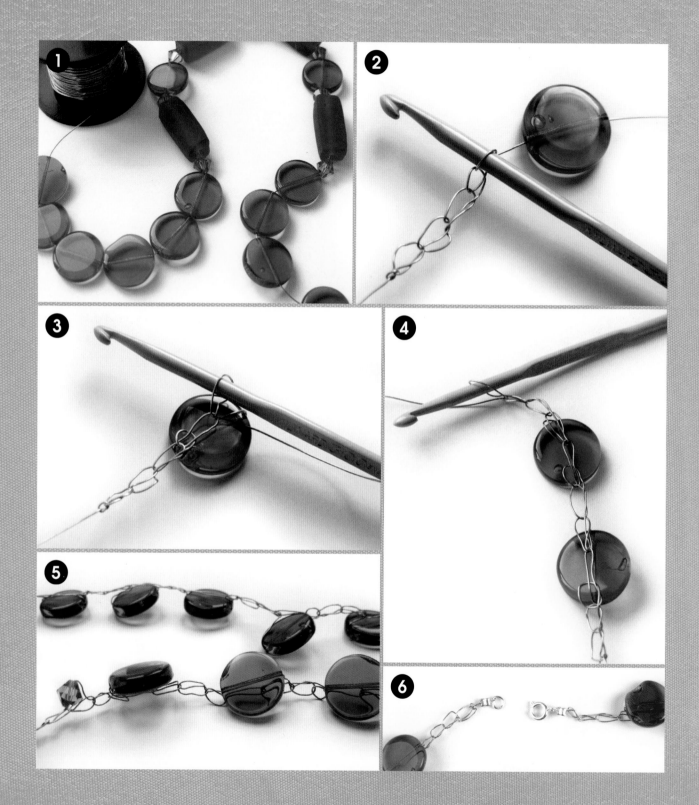

1 Before threading the beads, plan out your necklace on the table to ensure that each side matches. Thread the beads onto the wire.

2 Make a slip loop and work 4 chain.

3 Bring up the first bead and crochet a chain stitch to hold it in place. This may have to be a slightly larger stitch, depending on the size of the bead used. Don't let it get too big as the bead will then not stay in place.

4 Work 3 chain and then work next bead.

5 Repeat for the remainder of the beads. The chain stitches need to be worked evenly for the best results.

6 As you have only a single strand of wire at the finishing end, introduce another doubled piece to make it stronger before attaching the fastening.

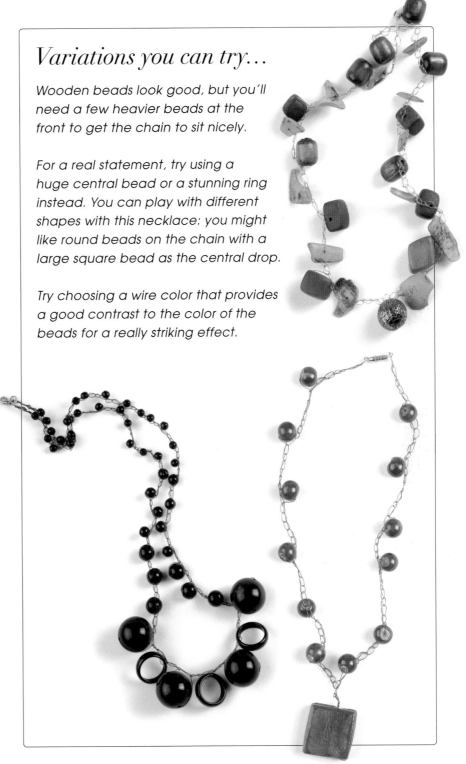

Variations you can try…

Wooden beads look good, but you'll need a few heavier beads at the front to get the chain to sit nicely.

For a real statement, try using a huge central bead or a stunning ring instead. You can play with different shapes with this necklace: you might like round beads on the chain with a large square bead as the central drop.

Try choosing a wire color that provides a good contrast to the color of the beads for a really striking effect.

Aqua

Crochet-covered beads

An unusual necklace that is great fun to make. Using just a simple chain stitch and a slip stitch will produce a unique work of art. The focus should be on the wire in this necklace, so I've chosen to use clear beads and colored wire.

You will need

65½ft (20m) of 0.2mm
(AWG 32, SWG 30) wire

3.25mm (USD-3:UK10),
or smaller, crochet hook

About 25 beads, ¾in (1.5cm)
in size

Fastening of your choice

For a professional finish…

Fine wire and a fine crochet hook work best for this necklace. Big beads are easier to use when you are doing this for the first time.

Don't worry too much about the tension of your chain stitches but do try to keep the ones between the beads even.

Try to cover the first holding stitch on the bead with crochet rather than leaving a strand of wire exposed.

1 Arrange the beads in a graduated row: place the largest ones in the center and work out to smaller ones at the 2 ends.

2 Thread the beads onto the wire.

3 Make a slip loop and work 4 chain.

4 Feed up the first bead and secure in place with a chain st.

5 Now work a few chain sts to go round the bead; how large you make the sts will depend on the size of the bead. Where the chains cross, work a slip st to secure. Continue crocheting and slip stitching until you are happy that there is enough wire around the bead. (The bead won't "escape" because it is threaded on to the wire.)

6 Work 2 or 3 chain to move on to the next bead. Repeat for the length of the necklace.

7 When you reach the end, work several chain sts to turn, then work back along the necklace, filling in any gaps

that have occurred. This will also double the chain between each bead, which gives it added strength.

8 Finish off and attach the fastening.

Variations you can try...

You can use big beads but it is best to crochet a length of chain before you start beading, particularly if you want the beads just in the middle of the necklace. Again, work a double row of crochet to make sure the beads have sufficient crochet over them. This also helps to add substance to the support chain.

Try putting small Swarovski beads on the wire before the big beads; you can also work these on the return chain. Another good effect can be achieved by working two different colors of wire.

Use as much crochet to cover the beads as you wish. Quite a different effect can be achieved with densely covered beads.

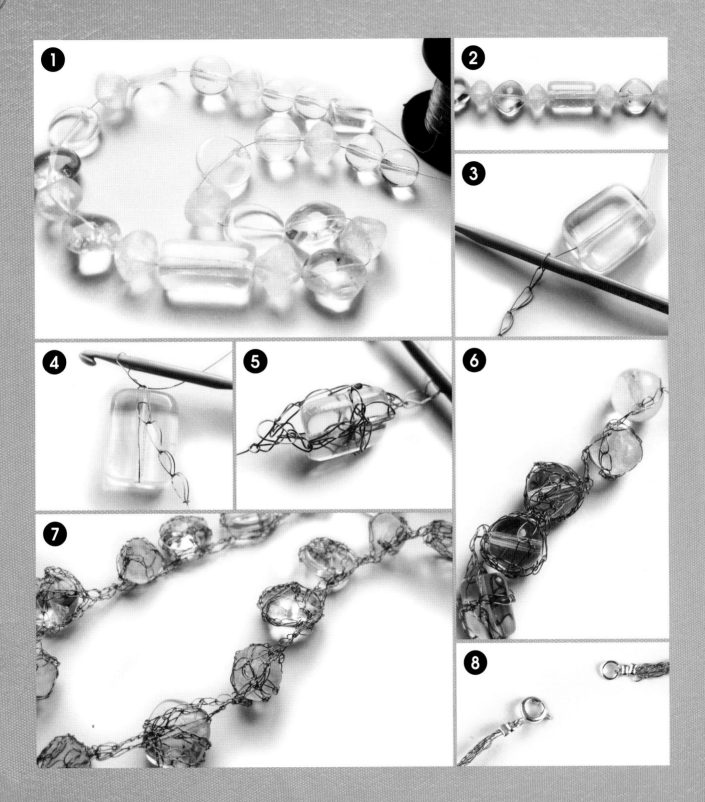

113

Leaf

Delicate-shaped chain

An attractive dainty-looking necklace that involves only two crochet stitches but produces stunning results. This necklace is very free in its construction, so each one is unique.

You will need

65½ft (20m) of 0.315mm(AWG 28, SWG 30) wire

2mm (USB-0:UK14) crochet hook

About 24 pearl beads

Fastening of your choice

For a professional finish…

Don't make the necklace too long—it works best as one that sits on the collar bone.

When working the chain stitch, keep it fairly loose to enable you to work the return single crochets. On the return row, you might need to work the odd chain stitch between the single crochet to keep your work flat.

The beads will all sit on the same side of the work as you progress. To get the bead to sit in the middle of the leaf, bead as you join to make the leaf shape.

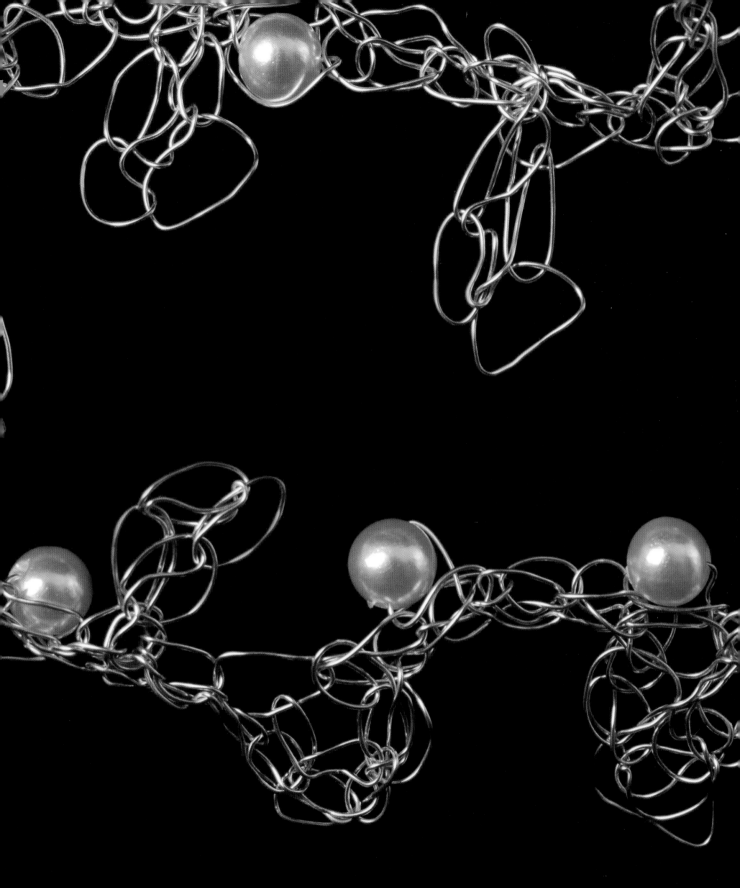

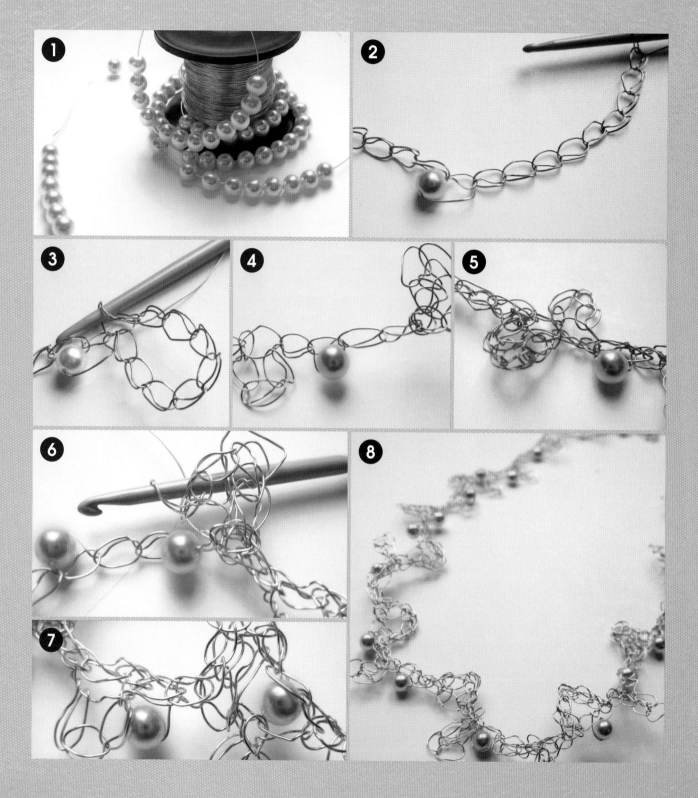

1 Thread the beads onto the wire.

2 Crochet 4 chain, then bead. Crochet 10 sts.

3 Come back on yourself and work a single crochet into the second chain after the bead. (This should then produce a leaf shape.)

4 Work 2 more chain, and bead again. Work 7 more chain. Then work a single crochet into the second chain after the bead but this time make the leaf fall on the other side of the necklace.

5 Continue in this manner beading and working leaf shapes on each side of the necklace. The leaves can be varied in size by the number of chain you work and do not have to follow symmetrically down the necklace. Bead as you wish, sometimes placing the beads in the chain between the leaves.

6 Continue for the required length of necklace. At the end, work about 6 chain to give you a good base for attaching the fastening. Then turn and work back along the necklace on the inside edge only working single crochet into the chain sts already worked. Where you meet a leaf shape work round this putting 2 single crochet into the top sts of the leaf. Pinch the work to flatten it as you work along.

7 If you want to add more beads as you work the return stitches, then do so.

8 Finish off when you reach the end, then flatten and ease the necklace into shape. Attach the fastening.

Variations you can try...

Use any small beads for this necklace—¼in (6mm) Swarovski beads would look good, or you could try black beads on black wire.

To make a wider necklace, make a third return row on the unworked side of the necklace. The necklace works very well as a choker, fastened with a ribbon that is beaded at the ends, and you can easily make matching earrings, too.

twisting

Twilight

Basic beaded twisting

This pretty necklace is very easy to make: you simply use twisting to hold the beads in place. It can be a single strand or a layered necklace and is very quick to do.

You will need

2 x 65½ft (20m) lengths of 0.2mm (AWG 32, SWG 36) wire in contrasting colors

About 60 small beads

A few larger central beads

Fastening of your choice

Crimp beads

For a professional finish…

Do not over twist as there is a risk of snapping the wire. Four or five twists between each bead should be enough and will give a gap of about ½in (1cm). It is best to use fine wire for this project since thicker wire can be a bit rigid.

Watch that you don't untwist a previous bead as you work the next one; keep checking as you go along. When you reach the end, work back along the necklace putting any twists that have come out back in place.

1 Thread the beads onto one of the lengths of wire.

2 Twist and then tie the 2 ends of the wire together. Holding some beads in your right hand, twist the 2 wires together, trapping a bead in place. Always twist in the same direction and ensure that the wire is actually twisting between each bead and that you are not just spinning the bead around.

3 Continue along the wire, spacing the beads evenly as you go.

4 When you have sufficient length of necklace, cut the wire ends, twist, and then tie a knot.

5 If you want to make a layered necklace, then work more strands of different lengths.

6 Use crimp beads to secure the strands together before attaching a fastening.

Variations you can try...

This versatile necklace can also be made as a single strand. You can use round or irregularly shaped beads depending on the effect that you want. You could add a large central bead, perhaps flagged by two smaller ones, for dramatic effect.

The piece can be made as a long continuous strand; simply join the ends without a fastening and then wear as a necklace or bracelet.

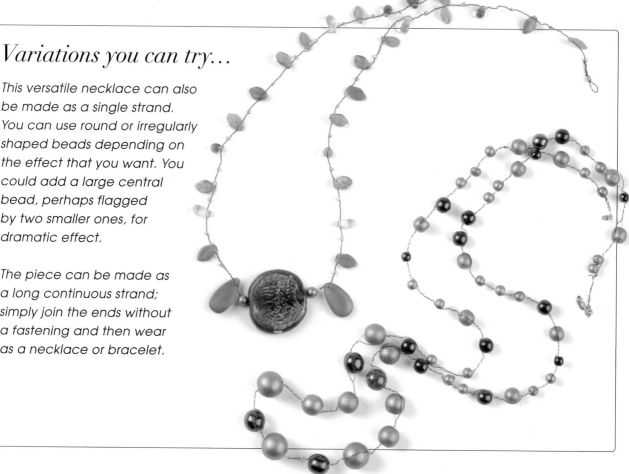

Tree

Branched-effect twisting

A pretty necklace that only requires twists to produce an interesting and unusual effect. Using a mixture of small beads, this necklace grows quickly, and produces a unique and attractive piece of jewelry.

You will need

98½ft (30m) of 0.25mm (AWG 30, SWG 33) wire

About 100 assorted small beads, ¼in (6mm) in size

Fastening of your choice

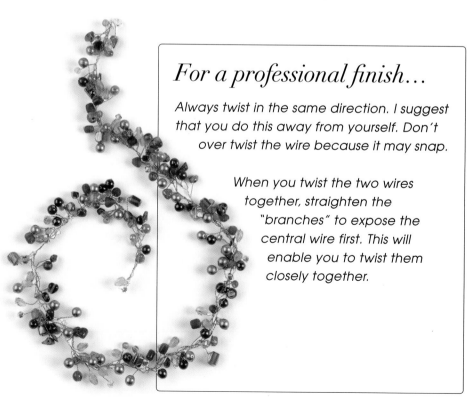

For a professional finish…

Always twist in the same direction. I suggest that you do this away from yourself. Don't over twist the wire because it may snap.

When you twist the two wires together, straighten the "branches" to expose the central wire first. This will enable you to twist them closely together.

1. Thread a mixture of beads onto the wire.

2. Pull about 6ft (2m) of wire off the reel and fold it back on itself so you have a double thickness of wire. Begin twisting the wire together leaving a little loop for attaching the fastening later.

3. Bring up a bead and form a little "branch" about ½in (1cm) long with the bead at the top.

4. Twist the wire away from you, fixing the bead at the end of the wire. Continue making the "branches" of varying lengths, twisting about ½in (1cm) of wire in between each one. (You should be using a double thickness of wire.)

5. Continue to the end of the wire—or beads. You need a length of necklace that is twice the required finished length. Then fold the work in half and twist the 2 halves together carefully.

6. Attach the fastening.

Variations you can try…

Using two different colors of beads looks good, or you could use four strands of twisted "trees" for a fuller necklace.

The method can be used for earrings; simply make a short length and attach to the findings.

Copper

Combined knot and twist

This is an easy but effective necklace. It is made with three strands of wire, which are first beaded and then twisted and knotted in place.

You will need

3 x 65½ft (20m) lengths of 0.2mm (AWG 32, SWG 36) fine wire, in toning colors.

150 assorted beads, about ³⁄₈in (8mm) in size

Fastening of your choice

For a professional finish…

Make the bead clusters different by varying the number of beads and their position.

The wire in the cluster doesn't need to be too tight: allowing the beads to chink against each other adds to the effect.

Don't tighten the knot until you are happy with its position and have made sure that the three wires are together. Wrap the knot around a finger to fix the wire loop.

① Thread about 50 beads onto each wire.

② Bring the 3 loose wire ends together and knot them. Bring up some beads from each wire to the knotted end.

③ Cluster the beads so they sit nicely and twist the wire after the cluster. Don't over twist or it will snap. Make a knot, using all 3 strands of wire, after the twist.

④ Repeat for the next cluster, twisting and then knotting to hold the beads in place. Try to make the length of twist and the position of the knot the same between each cluster. About 5 twists should be enough.

⑤ Continue for the required length, then tie a final knot.

⑥ Attach the fastening.

Variations you can try...

Using wire and beads of contrasting colors creates a fun-looking and striking necklace. Try making the central clusters noticeably bigger for an interesting effect; you could also use different center beads.

You can make a matching bracelet using the same basic method, but you will need to position the clusters closer together than for the necklace.

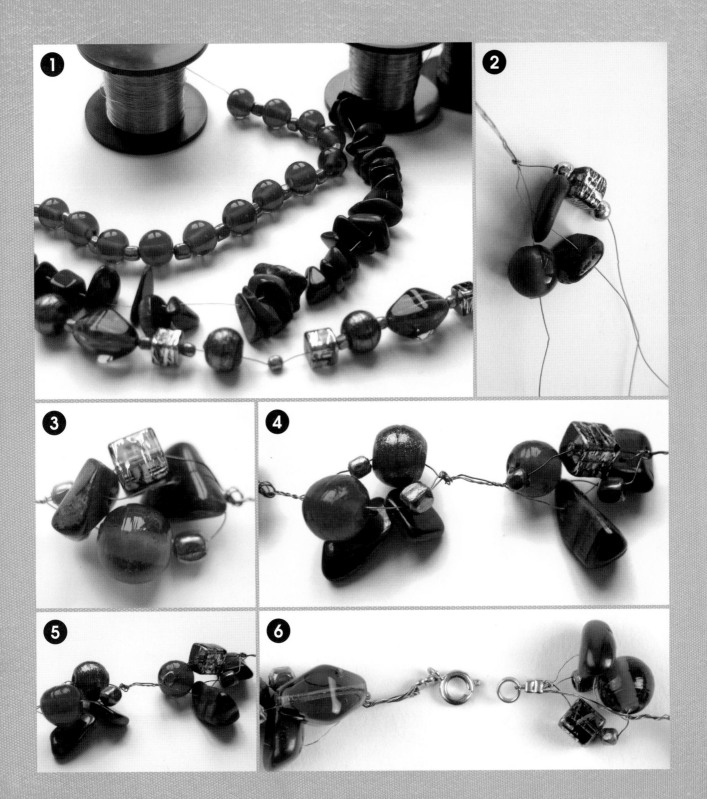

Cochineal

Basic twisted coil

This unusual necklace is quick and easy to make yet has a dramatic impact. A simple twisting technique is all you need to make this attractive design.

You will need

2 x 65½ (20m) lengths of 0.315 mm wire (AWG 28: SWG 30)

3.25mm (US-3:UK10) long knitting needle

6 crimp beads

Fastening of your choice

For a professional finish…

Check that the central bead will fit. Push the knitting needle you intend to wrap around through the hole in the bead; it should fit loosely.

If the hole in the bead is too small, don't worry. Use the central support wire to attach the bead where you want it. Bring it out through the coil in the right place, go through the bead, then return inside the coil. Use 0.315mm (AWG 28, SWG 30) wire.

If the coil is too long, simply push it up the support wire before crimping. Avoid stretching the coil as it will lose its shape.

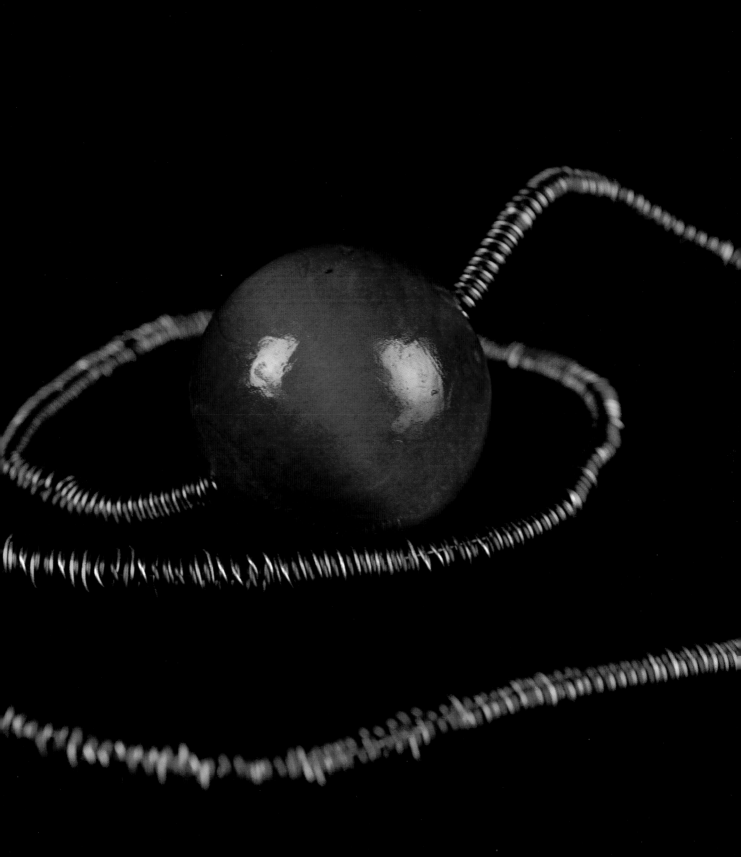

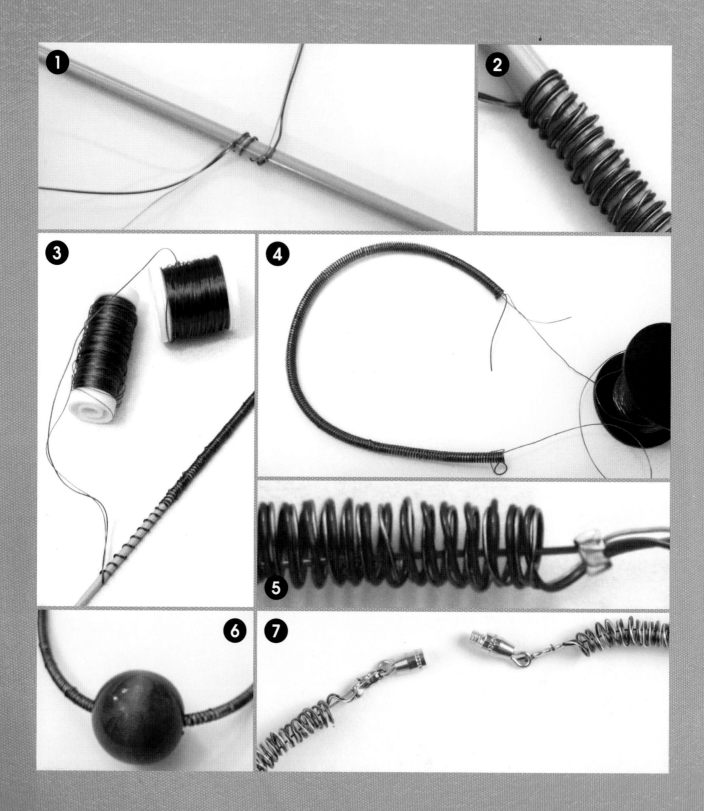

1 Hold the ends of the wire together and begin twisting tightly around the knitting needle. When twisting, turn the needle not the reels as this gives you better control.

2 Push the wire together as you work, ensuring that there are no overlapping twists. Avoid creating kinks in the wire as they will show.

3 Continue with this method until the needle is covered with compacted twists.

4 Slide the work off the needle. Cut the reel ends of the wire. With a strand of wire from 1 of the reels, push it along the center of the coil.

5 When the wire emerges at the end of the coil, use a crimp bead to secure all 3 wires together—the 2 from the coil and the central one together. Finish the other end in a similar way. Just check the length of the necklace and adjust before you cut the reel end off. The

necklace can be shortened if needed by pushing the coils closer together.

6 Feed a large holed bead along the coil.

7 Attach the fastenings.

Variations you can try...

Be brave with colors and experiment with different combinations on little test pieces. You can use three colors rather than just two; you can use a lighter wire if you are using three colors.

You can make a necklace with layers of coils. Make sure the central beads fit together well.

For earrings, use a thinner needle and leave a ¾in (2cm) tail of wire for finishing. Make 2¾in (7cm) of compacted coil. Bend the finishing wire at 90 degrees to the coil. Feed the ends through a crimp bead to secure and attach fastenings. Earrings don't need a support wire but a bracelet does.

Blossom

Spiral-effect coil

This necklace develops the skills learned in the previous project, and produces a versatile and attractive necklace that can take many forms.

You will need

65½ft (20m) of 0.315mm (AWG 28, SWG 30) wire

2mm (US-0:UK14) knitting needle

Selection of Swarovski and larger enamel beads

Fastening of your choice

For a professional finish…

Make sure that you go through the center of the coil bead when threading. It is easy to miss the twists at the end of the bead and then it won't sit properly on the wire. Take care to tuck the tails of wire on each coil bead well out of the way. Use pointed pliers to turn the ends inside the initial and end twists.

Attach one half of the fastening to the loose end of wire before you cut off the reel end. This keeps the beads from escaping.

1 Wrap the wire tightly round the needle. Twist the needle rather than the reel of wire, and don't let the wire overlap on the needle.

2 Continue until the wrapped wire measures 1¾in (4.5cm) when compacted. Avoid kinks, which spoil the bead; start again rather than try to correct the problem.

3 Snip the reel end and twist tightly once more to make sure the wire lies flat against the needle. Make all the coils you need now so they measure the same length.

4 Feed the loose end of the reel through the coil.

5 Hold the loose end of the wire against the needle and wrap it around about 8 times.

6 Bring the coil up the wire and carefully wrap this around the needle.

7 Wrap the reel wire around the needle so it matches the other end.

8 Hold the knitting needle in both hands and gently push the opposite ends of the work together to compact the wire-coil bead. Slide it off the needle. Repeat to make 12 beads.

9 Feed the wire-coil beads onto a length of wire, including the Swarovski and enamel beads as required. Attach the fastening.

Variations you can try...

Use a larger needle, and wrap the wire more times around it to make a larger coiled bead. You can also make longer coils, and use fewer beads in between them. A heavier wire can be used if you are doing this.

For a matching bracelet, use slightly shorter wire-coil beads and experiment with placing a few differently shaped beads in between them. If you want earrings, use a single short coil for each one, and add beads if needed.

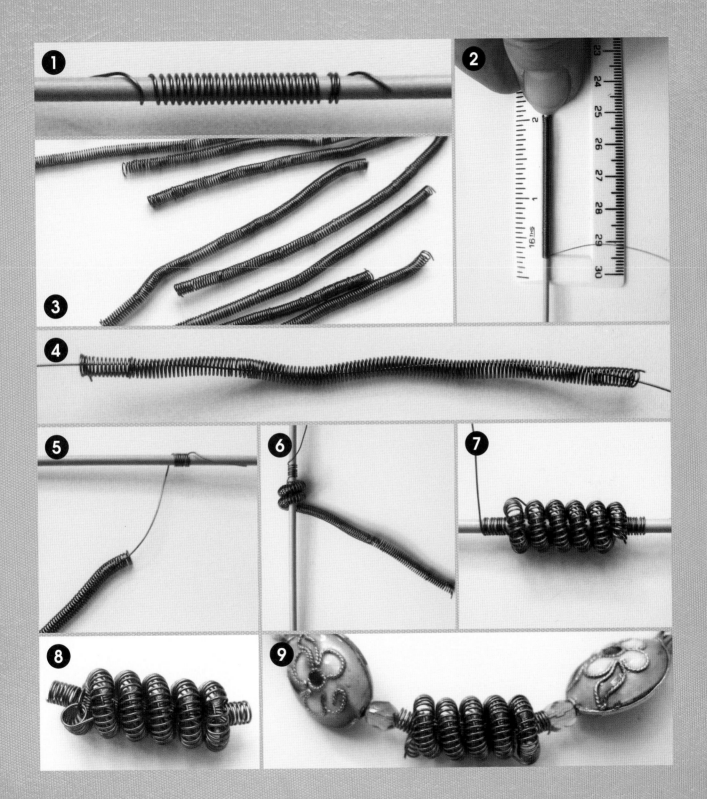

Conversions

WIRE CONVERSION CHARTS

Wire can be measured either by gauge or diameter. These charts show the approximate metric conversion of the American Wire Gauge (AWG) and the Standard Wire Gauge (SWG).

American Wire Gauge (AWG)	Equivalent in mm
33	0.18
32	0.20
31	0.22
30	0.25
29	0.29
28	0.32
27	0.36
26	0.40
25	0.45
24	0.51
23	0.57
22	0.64
21	0.72
20	0.81
19	0.91
18	1.02

Standard Wire Gauge (SWG)	Equivalent in mm
38	0.15
37	0.17
36	0.19/0.20
35	0.21
34	0.23
33	0.25
32	0.27
31	0.29
30	0.30/0.31
29	0.34
28	0.37
27	0.41
26	0.45
25	0.5
24	0.59
23	0.61
22	0.71
21	0.81
20	0.91
19	1.01
18	1.21

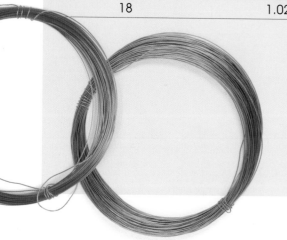

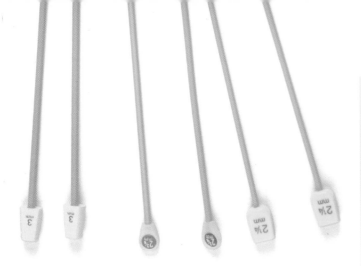

CROCHET HOOK SIZES

Metric (mm)	US	UK
10	P-15	000
9	N-13	00
8	L-11	0
7	K-10 1/22	
6.5	10 1/4	3
6	J-10	4
5.5	I-9	5
5	H-8	6
4.5	7	7
4	G-6	8
3.75	F-5	9
3.5	E-4	9
3.25	D-3	10
2.75	C-2	12
2.25	B-1	13
2	B-0	14

KNITTING NEEDLE SIZES

Metric (mm)	US	UK
2	0	14
2.25	1	13
2.75	2	12
3	–	11
3.25	3	10
3.5	4	–
3.75	5	9
4	6	8
4.5	7	7
5	8	6
5.5	9	5
6	10	4
6.5	10.5	3
7	–	2
7.5	–	1
8	11	0
9	13	00
10	15	000

UK/US TERMS

UK	US
Double crochet	Single crochet
Half treble	Half double crochet
Treble	Double crochet
Cast off	Bind off

141

Suppliers

There are many different suppliers for jewelry materials online. There are also a number of sellers on auction sites (have a close look at their feedback before you order). Here are some web addresses that you may find useful.

UK

www.beadsdirect.co.uk
www.beadsunlimited.co.uk
www.creativebeadcraft.co.uk
www.justbeads.co.uk
www.the-beadshop.co.uk
www.scattercrystals.co.uk
www.wires.co.uk

US

www.firemountaingems.com
www.find-beads.com
www.dibeads.com
www.jsbeads.com
www.beadaholique.com
www.susiesbeads.com
www.ibead.com

CANADA

www.beadfx.com
www.thebeadingroom.com
www.mydreambeads.com
www.ahbeads.com
www.jewelrysupply.com
www.canbead.com
www.rainbowbeadsonline.com

AUSTRALIA

www.spacetrader.com.au
www.uniquebeads.com.au
www.empirebeads.com.au
www.beadcharm.com.au
www.beadandcrystalheaven.com.au
www.beadneeds.com.au
www.mybeads.com.au

AUTHOR'S WEB SITE

www.kathorsman.com

OTHER SOURCES

Jewelry-making magazines often have a section at the back, where a large number of sellers advertize. *Making Jewellery* magazine, published by GMC Publications has a comprehensive guide.

It is also worth looking in thrift stores. You can often find short knitting needles, crochet hooks, and beads to use.

When ordering beads, have a look to see if the supplier does large 35oz (1kg) bags of mixed glass beads (sometimes called sweepings), which are particularly good value. When buying beads online, check the size carefully as pictures can be deceptive.

Index

To place an order, or to request a catalogue, contact:
GMC Publications Ltd, Castle Place, 166 High Street,
Lewes, East Sussex BN7 1XU United Kingdom
Tel: +44 (0)1273 488005 Fax: +44 (0)1273 402866
www.gmcbooks.com